Henry Morley, Plato

Crito and Phaedo

Dialogues of Socrates before his Death

Henry Morley, Plato

Crito and Phaedo

Dialogues of Socrates before his Death

ISBN/EAN: 9783337395605

Printed in Europe, USA, Canada, Australia, Japan

Cover: Foto ©Thomas Meinert / pixelio.de

More available books at **www.hansebooks.com**

PLATO'S

CRITO AND PHÆDO.

*Dialogues of Socrates before his
Death.*

CASSELL & COMPANY, Limited:
LONDON, PARIS, NEW YORK & MELBOURNE.
1888.

INTRODUCTION.

SOCRATES lives for us in the works of Plato as the loftiest expression of the spiritual life of ancient Greece. Plato, a philosopher with the mind of a poet, was able to feel and to share the aspirations of his teacher, and gave in dialogues a half-dramatic expression of the personality and of the doctrines of the man who wrote no book himself, but whose best wisdom is enshrined in the works of two great writers who drew strength from his friendship—Xenophon and Plato.

Socrates, the son of Sophroniscus, a sculptor, was born just outside Athens in the year 468 B.C. —more than two thousand three hundred and fifty years ago. He studied life by communion with men, loved Athens, and, when young, fought in her battles. But he avoided political conflict, because he resolved to devote his life to the awakening of the best powers of men for the battle towards a higher life than that he saw around him. Without teaching formally in any school, he seized every opportunity he found of lifting the thoughts of old and young with whom he came in contact in the workshops, or in the gymnasium, in their homes, or in the marketplace. He sought to make them look straight down into themselves, see clearly what they thought they knew, and then rise to the height of their best aspirations, " knighted from kneeling."

Socrates had no faith in the wisdom of the multitude, and while he exhorted men to worship the gods in the form ordained by the state, his spiritual teaching all pointed to one great First Cause in a way that drew attention from religious symbols to the soul of truth that they embodied. He was attacked, therefore, by politicians and by priests. Condemned as an innovator, by a majority of six votes, he justified himself instead of pleading against a heavy sentence. Sentenced then by a majority of eighty votes to death, he declared that he would rather die because he had defended himself honestly, than live because he had appealed to pity. For thirty days after his sentence, Socrates lived in prison conversing with his friends, because a law forbade executions during the time of the annual voyage of the sacred ship, the *Theoris*, with offerings to the shrine at Delos. The dialogues in this volume represent the reasonings of Socrates in the last hours of his life, in the year 399 B.C., when his age was seventy.

Plato was born at Athens in the year 430 B.C., and was, therefore, thirty-one years old at the time of the death of Socrates. He was born of a distinguished family; his rare gift of genius was aided by the most liberal culture, and at the age of twenty he became the devoted follower of Socrates. After the death of Socrates, he and other disciples of the Master went, for safety, to Megara.

Crito, whom Plato represents in dialogue with Socrates immediately before the return of the sacred ship, was a very rich Athenian who was devoted to Socrates, and who himself wrote seventeen philosophical dialogues, which are now lost. He used his wealth in doing good; kept Socrates free from care about means of subsistence, and had made all arrangements for his escape from death, as is shown here in Plato's dialogue of Duty, which bears the name of Crito.

Phædo, who gives his name to the closing dialogue of Immortality, was a philosopher, born of a good family at Elis, who was taken prisoner in war, and brought as a slave to Athens about a year before the death of Socrates. It was as a slave that he first talked with the Master to whom he became devoted. Other disciples of Socrates purchased Phædo's freedom. He was then a beautiful youth scarcely eighteen years old, for he still wore the long hair that it was usual to cut short at eighteen. He was received kindly by the friends of Socrates, and we see how Plato gives him prominence in that last dialogue of Immortality—the other dialogue in this volume—which has been often said to paint to us the Christian before Christ. The reader will not fail to observe that when Plato records as the last words of Socrates the reminder that he owed a cock to Æsculapius, his purpose is to show that, however Socrates was accused of neglect of the gods, he was punctual in observance of the religious rites by which his countrymen declared that they could lift their eyes above the earth on which they trod.

The translation here given of the "Crito" and the "Phædo" is one that was published in 1783, a year before the death of Samuel Johnson.

H. M.

CRITO;
OR, OF WHAT WE OUGHT TO DO.

SOCRATES and CRITO.

Soc. What's the occasion of your coming here so soon, Crito? As I take it, 'tis very early.

Crit. Indeed it is.

Soc. What o'clock may it be then?

Crit. A little before the break of day.

Soc. I wonder that the gaoler permitted you to come in.

Crit. He is one I know very well. I have been with him here frequently; and he is in some measure obliged to me.

Soc. Are you but just come? Or is it long since you came?

Crit. I have been here a good while.

Soc. Why did you not awaken me then when you came in?

Crit. Pray God forbid, Socrates. For my own part, I would gladly shake off the cares and anxiety that keep my eyes from shutting. But when I entered this room, I wondered to find you so sound asleep, and was loth to awaken you, that I might not deprive you of those happy minutes. Indeed, Socrates, ever since I became acquainted with you, I have been always delighted with your patience and calm temper: but in a distinguishing manner in this juncture, since, in the circumstances you are in, your eye looks so easy and unconcerned.

Soc. Indeed, Crito, it would be very unbecoming in one of my age to be fearful of death.

Crit. Ay! And how many do we see every day, under the like misfortunes, whom age does not free from those dreads?

Soc. That is true. But after all what made you come hither so early?

Crit. I came to tell you a perplexing piece of news, which, though it may not seem to affect you, yet it overwhelms both me and your relations and friends with insupportable grief. In short, I bring the most terrible news that ever could be brought.

Soc. What news? Is the ship arrived from Delos, upon whose return I am to die?

Crit. It is not yet arrived; but doubtless it will be here this day, according to the intelligence we have from some persons that came from Sunium, and left it there. For at that rate it cannot fail of being here to-day; and to-morrow you must unavoidably die.

Soc. Why not, Crito? Be it so, since 'tis the will of God. However, I do not think that the vessel will arrive this day.

Crit. What do you ground that conjecture upon?

Soc. I'll tell you: I am not to die till the day after the arrival of the vessel.

Crit. At least, those who are to execute the sentence say so.

Soc. That vessel will not arrive till to-morrow, as I conjecture from a certain dream I had this night about a minute ago. And it seems to me a pleasure that you did not awaken me.

Crit. Well, what is this dream?

Soc. I thought I saw a very gentle comely woman, dressed in white, come up to me, who calling me by name, said, "In three days thou shalt be in the fertile Phthia."

Crit. That is a very remarkable dream, Socrates.

Soc. 'Tis a very significant one, Crito.

Crit. Yes, without doubt. But for this time, prithee, Socrates, take my advice, and make your escape. For my part, if you die, besides the irreparable loss of a friend, which I shall ever bewail, I am afraid that numbers of people, who are not well acquainted either with you or me, will believe that I have forsaken you, in not employing my interest for promoting your escape, now that it is in my power. Is there anything more base than to lie under the disrepute of being wedded to my money more than to my friend? For, in fine, the people will never believe that 'twas you who refused to go from hence, when we urged you to be gone.

Soc. My dear Crito, why should we be so much concerned for the opinion of the people? Is it not enough that the more sensible part, who are the only men we ought to regard, know how the case stands?

Crit. But you see, Socrates, there's a necessity of being concerned for the noise of the mob; for your example is sufficient instance that they are capable of doing, not only small, but the greatest of injuries, and display their passion in an outrageous manner against those who are once run down by the vulgar opinion.

Soc. I wish, Crito, that the people were able to do the greatest of injuries. Were it so, they would likewise be capable of doing the greatest good. That would be a great happiness. But neither the one nor the other is possible. For they cannot make men either wise men or fools.

Crit. I grant it. But pray answer me: Is it out of tenderness to me and your other friends that you will not stir from hence? Is it fear lest upon your escape we should be troubled, and charged with carrying you off, and by that means be obliged to quit our possession, or pay a large sum of money, or else suffer something more fatal than either? If that be your fear, shake it off, Socrates, in the name of the gods. Is not it highly reasonable that we should purchase your escape at the rate of exposing ourselves to these dangers, and greater ones, if there be occasion? Once more, my dear Socrates, believe me, and go along with me.

Soc. I own, Crito, that I have such thoughts, and several others besides in my view.

Crit. Fear nothing, I entreat you; for, in the first place, they require no great sum to let you out. And on the other hand, you see what a pitiful condition those are in who probably might arraign us. A small sum of money will stop their mouths: my estate alone will serve for that. If you scruple to accept of my offer, here are a great many strangers who desire nothing more than to furnish you with what money you want. Simmias the Theban himself has brought up very considerable sums. Cebes is capable of doing as much, and so are several others. Let not your fears then stifle the desire of making your escape. And as for what you told me the other day, in court, that if you made your escape, you should not know how to live—pray let not that trouble you. Whithersoever you go, you'll be beloved in all parts of the world. If you'll go to Thessaly, I have friends there, who will honour you according to your merit, and think themselves happy in supplying you with what you want, and covering you from all occasions of fear in their country. Besides, Socrates, without doubt you are guilty of a very unjust thing in delivering up yourself, while 'tis in your power to make your escape, and promoting what your enemies so passionately wish for. For you not only betray yourself, but likewise your children by abandoning them, when you might make a shift to maintain and educate them. You are not at all concerned at what may befall them, though at the same time they are like to be in as dismal a condition as ever poor orphans were. A man ought either to have no children, or else to expose himself to the care and trouble of breeding them. You seem to me to act the softest and most insensible part in the world; whereas you ought to take up a resolution worthy of a generous soul; above all, you who boast that you pursued nothing but virtue all the days of your life. I tell you, Socrates, I am ashamed upon the account of you and your relations, since the world will believe 'twas owing to our cowardliness that you did not get off. In the first place, they will charge you with standing a trial that you might have avoided; then they will censure your conduct in making your defences; and at last, which is the most shameful of all, they will upbraid us with forsaking you through fear or cowardice, since we did not accomplish your escape. Pray consider of it, my dear Socrates; if you do not prevent the approaching evil, you'll bear a part in the shame that will cover us all. Pray advise with yourself quickly. But now I think on it, there is not time for advising, there's no choice left, all must be put in execution.

Soc. My dear Crito, your good-will is very commendable, provided it agree with right reason; but if it swerve from that, the stronger it is, the more is it blameworthy. The first thing to be considered is, whether we ought to do as you say, or not? For you know, 'tis not of yesterday that

I've accustomed myself only to follow the reasons that appear most just after a mature examination. Though fortune frowns upon me, yet I'll never part with the principles I have all along professed. These principles appear always the same, and I esteem them equally at all times. So, if your advice be not backed by the strongest reasons, assure yourself I will never comply, not if all the power of the people should arm itself against me, or offer to frighten me like a child, by laying on fresh chains, and threatening to deprive me of the greatest good, and oblige me to suffer the cruellest death.

Crit. Now, how shall we manage this inquiry justly?

Soc. To be sure, the fairest way is to resume what you have been saying of the vulgar opinions; that is, to inquire whether there are some reports that we ought to regard, and others that are to be slighted; or, whether the saying so is only a groundless and childish proposition. I have a strong desire, upon this occasion, to try, in your presence, whether this principle will appear to me in different colours from what it did while I was in other circumstances, or whether I shall always find it the same, in order to determine me to compliance or refusal.

If I mistake not, 'tis certain that several persons, who thought themselves men of sense, have often maintained in this place, that of all the opinions of men, some are to be regarded and others to be slighted. In the name of the gods, Crito, do not you think that was well said? In all human appearance you are in no danger of dying to-morrow; and therefore 'tis presumed that the fear of the present danger cannot work any change upon you. Wherefore, pray consider it well: do not you think they spoke justly who said that all the opinions of men are not always to be regarded, but only some of them; and those not of all men, but only of some? What do you say? Do not you think 'tis very true?

Crit. Very true.

Soc. At any rate, then, ought not we to esteem the good opinions and slight the bad ones?

Crit. Ay, doubtless.

Soc. Are not the good opinions then those of wise men, and the bad ones those of fools?

Crit. It cannot be otherwise.

Soc. Let us see, then, how you will answer this. A man who makes his exercises, when he comes to have his lesson, whether shall he regard the commendation or censure of whoever comes first, or only of him that is either a physician or a master?

Crit. Of the last, to be sure.

Soc. Then he ought to fear the censure and value the commendation of that man alone, and slight what comes from others.

Crit. Without doubt.

Soc. For that reason this young man must neither eat nor drink, nor do anything, without the orders of that master, that man of sense, and he is not at all to govern himself by the caprices of others.

Crit. That is true.

Soc. Let us fix upon that, then. But suppose he disobeys this master, and disregards his applause or censure, and suffers himself to be blinded by the caresses and applauses of the ignorant mob, will not he come to some harm by this means?

Crit. How is it possible it should be otherwise?

Soc. But what will be the nature of this harm that will accrue to him thereupon? where will it terminate? and what part of him will it affect?

Crit. His body, without doubt; for by that means he'll ruin himself.

Soc. Very well, but is not the case the same all over? Upon the point of justice or injustice, honesty or dishonesty, good or evil, which at present are the subject of our dispute, shall we rather refer ourselves to the opinion of the people than to that of an experienced wise man, who justly challenges more respect and deference from us than all the world besides? And if we do not act conformably to the opinion of this one man, is it not certain that we shall ruin ourselves, and entirely lose that which only lives and gains new strength by justice, and perishes only through injustice? Or must we take all that for a thing of no account?

Crit. I am of your opinion.

Soc. Take heed, I entreat you; if, by following

the opinions of the ignorant, we destroy that which is only preserved by health and wasted by sickness, can we survive the corruption of that, whether it be our body or somewhat else?

Crit. That's certain.

Soc. Can one live then after the corruption and destruction of the body?

Crit. No, to be sure.

Soc. But can one survive the corruption of that which lives only by justice, and dies only through injustice? Or is this thing (whatever it be) that has justice or injustice for its object, to be less valued than the body?

Crit. Not at all.

Soc. What, is it much more valuable then?

Crit. A great deal more.

Soc. Then, my dear Crito, we ought not to be concerned at what the people say, but what he says, who knows what is just and unjust; and that alone is nothing else but the truth. Thus you see you established false principles at first, in saying that we ought to pay a deference to the opinions of the people upon what is just, good, honest, and its contraries. Some, perhaps, will object that the people are able to put us to death.

Crit. To be sure they will start that objection.

Soc. 'Tis also true. But that does not alter the nature of what we were saying; that is still the same. For you must still remember that 'tis not life, but a good life, that we ought to court.

Crit. That is a certain truth.

Soc. But is it not likewise certain that this good life consists in nothing else but honesty and justice?

Crit. Yes.

Soc. Now, before we go farther, let us examine, upon the principles you have agreed to, whether my departure from hence, without the permission of the Athenians, is just or unjust. If it be found just, we must do our utmost to bring it about; but if it be unjust, we must lay aside the design. For as to the considerations you alleged just now of money, reputation, and family, these are only the thoughts of the baser mob, who put innocent persons to death, and would afterwards bring them to life if 'twere possible. But as for us who bend our thoughts another way, all that we are to mind is whether we do a just thing in giving money, and lying under an obligation to those who promote our escape ; or whether both we and they do not commit a piece of injustice in so doing? If this be an unjust thing, we need not reason much upon the point, since 'tis better to abide here and die than to undergo somewhat more terrible than death.

Crit. You are in the right, Socrates ; let us see then how it will fall.

Soc. We shall go hand in hand in the inquiry. If you have anything of weight to answer, pray do it when I have spoken, that so I may comply ; if not, pray forbear any farther to press me to go hence without the consent of the Athenians. I shall be infinitely glad if you can persuade me to do it; but I cannot do it without being first convinced. Take notice then whether my way of pursuing this inquiry satisfies you, and do your utmost to make answer to my questions.

Crit. I will.

Soc. Is it true that we ought not to do an unjust thing to any man? Or is it lawful in any measure to do it to one when we are forbidden to do it to another? Or is it not absolutely true that all manner of injustice is neither good nor honest, as we were saying but now? Or, in fine, are all these sentiments which we formerly entertained, vanished in a few days? And is it possible, Crito, that those of years, our most serious conferences, should resemble those of children, and we at the same time not be sensible that 'tis so? Ought not we rather to stand to what we have said, as being a certain truth, that all injustice is scandalous and fatal to the person that commits it, let men say what they will, and let our fortune be never so good or bad?

Crit. That's certain.

Soc. Then must we avoid the least measure of injustice?

Crit. Most certainly.

Soc. Since we are to avoid the least degree of it, then we ought not to do it to those who are unjust to us, notwithstanding that this people think it lawful?

Crit. So I think.

Soc. But what! Ought we to do evil or not?

Crit. Without doubt we ought not.

Soc. But is it justice to repay evil with evil, pursuant to the opinion of the people, or is it unjust?

Crit. 'Tis highly unjust.

Soc. Then there's no difference between doing evil and being unjust?

Crit. I own it.

Soc. Then we ought not to do the least evil or injustice to any man, let him do by us as he will. But take heed, Crito, that by this concession you do not speak against your own sentiments. For I know very well there are few that will go this length: and 'tis impossible for those who vary in their sentiments upon this point to agree well together. Nay, on the contrary, the contempt of one another's opinions leads them to a reciprocal contempt of one another's persons. Consider well then if you are of the same opinion with me; and let us ground our reasonings upon this principle, that we ought not to do evil for evil, or treat those unjustly who are unjust to us.

For my part, I never did, nor ever will, entertain any other principle. Tell me then if you have changed your mind; if not, give ear to what follows.

Crit. I give ear.

Soc. Well: a man that has made a just promise, ought he to keep it, or to break it?

Crit. He ought to keep it.

Soc. If I go hence without the consent of the Athenians, shall not I injure some people, and especially those who do not deserve it? Or shall we in this follow what we think equally just to everybody?

Crit. I cannot answer you, for I do not understand you.

Soc. Pray take notice; when we put ourselves in a way of making our escape, or going hence, or how you please to call it, suppose the law and the republic should present themselves in a body before us, and accost us in this manner: "Socrates, what are you going to do? To put in execution what you now design, were wholly to ruin the laws and the state. Do you think a city can subsist when justice has not only lost its force, but is likewise perverted, overturned, and trampled under foot by private persons?" What answer could we make to such and many other questions? For what is it that an orator cannot say upon the overturning of that law which provides that sentences once pronounced shall not be infringed? Shall we answer, that the republic has judged amiss, and passed an unjust sentence upon us? Shall that be our answer?

Crit. Ah, without any scruple, Socrates.

Soc. What will the laws say then? "Socrates, is it not true that you agreed with us to submit yourself to a public trial?" And if we should seem to be surprised at such language, they'll continue, perhaps, "Be not surprised, Socrates, but make an answer, for you yourself used to insist upon question and answer. Tell then what occasion you have to complain of the republic and of us, that you are so eager upon destroying it? Are not we the authors of your birth? Is it not by our means that your father married her who brought you forth? What fault can you find with the laws we have established as to marriage?" "Nothing at all," should I answer. "As to the nourishing and bringing up of children, and the manner of your education, are not the laws just that we enacted upon that head, by which we obliged your father to bring you up to music and the exercises?" "Very just," I'd say. "Since you were born, brought up, and educated under our influence, durst you maintain that you are not our nursed child and subject as well as your father? And if you are, do you think to have equal power with us, as if it were lawful for you to inflict upon us all we enjoin you to undergo? But since you cannot lay claim to any such right against your father or your master, so as to repay evil for evil, injury for injury, how can you think to obtain that privilege against your country and the laws, insomuch that if we endeavour to put you to death, you'll counteract us, by endeavouring to prevent us and to ruin your country and its law? Can you call such an action just, you that are an inseparable follower of true virtue? Are you ignorant that your country is more considerable, and more worthy of respect and veneration before God and man than your father, mother, and all your relations together? That you ought to honour your country, yield to it, and humour it more than an angry father? That you must either reclaim it by your counsel, or obey its injunctions, and suffer without grumbling all that it imposes upon you? If it orders you to be whipped, or laid in irons, if it sends you to the wars, there to spend your blood, you ought to do it without demurring; you must not shake off the yoke, or flinch or quit your post; but in the army, in prison, and everywhere else, ought equally to obey the orders of your country, or else assist it with wholesome counsel. For if offering violence to a father or mother be a piece of grand impiety, to put force upon one's country is a much greater." What shall we answer to all this, Crito? Shall we acknowledge the truth of what the laws advance?

Crit. How can we avoid it?

Soc. " Do you see, then, Socrates," continue they, " what reason we have to brand your enterprise against us as unjust? Of us you hold your birth, your maintenance, your education; in fine, we have done you all the good we are capable of, as well as the other citizens. Indeed, we do not fail to make public proclamation, that 'tis lawful for every private man, if he does not find his account in the laws and customs of our republic, after a mature examination, to retire with all his effects whither he pleases. And if any of you cannot comply with our customs, and desires to remove and live elsewhere, not one of us shall hinder him, he may go where he pleases. But on the other hand, if any one of you continues to live here, after he has considered our way of administering justice, and the policy observed in the state, then, we say, he is in effect obliged to obey all our commands, and we maintain that his disobedience is unjust on a three-fold account: for not obeying those to whom he owes his birth; for trampling under foot those that educated him; and for violating his faith after he engaged to obey us, and not taking the pains to make remonstrances to us, if we happen to do any unjust thing. For notwithstanding that we only propose things without using any violence to procure obedience, and give every man his choice whether to obey us, or reclaim us by his counsel or remonstrances, yet he does neither the one nor the other. And we maintain, Socrates, that if you execute what you are now about, you will stand charged with all these crimes, and that in a much higher degree than if another private man had committed the same injustice." If I asked them the reason, without doubt they would stop my mouth by telling me that I submitted myself in a distinguishing · manner to all these conditions. "And we," continue they, "have great evidence that you were always pleased with us and the republic; for if this city had not been more agreeable to you than any other, you had never continued in it, no more than the other Athenians. None of the shows could ever tempt you to go out of the city, except once, that you went to see the games at the Isthmus: you never went anywhere else, excepting your military expeditions, and never undertook a voyage, as others are wont to do.

You never had the curiosity to visit other cities, or inquire after other laws, as being contented with us and our republic. You always made a distinguishing choice of us, and on all occasions testified that you submitted with all your heart to live according to our maxims. Besides, your having had children in this city is an infallible evidence that you like it. In fine, in this very last juncture you might have been sentenced to banishment if you would, and might then have done, with the consent of the republic, what you now attempt without their permission. But you were so stately, so unconcerned at death, that in your own terms you preferred death to banishment. But now you have no regard to these fine words, you are no further concerned for the laws, since you are going to overturn them. You do just what a pitiful slave would offer to do, by endeavouring to make your escape contrary to the laws of the treaty you have signed, by which you obliged yourself to live according to our rules. Pray answer us: Did not we say right in affirming that you agreed to this treaty, and submitted yourself to these terms, not only in words but in deeds?" What shall we say to all this, Crito? And what can we do else but acknowledge that 'tis so?

Crit. How can we avoid it, Socrates?

Soc. "What else then," continue they, "is this action of yours but a violation of that treaty, and all its terms? That treaty that you were not made to sign either by force or surprise, not without time to think on it: for you had the whole course of seventy years to have removed in, if you had been dissatisfied with us, or unconvinced of the justice of our proposals. You neither pitched upon Lacedæmon nor Crete, notwithstanding that you always cried up their laws; nor any of the other Grecian cities, or strange countries. You have been less out of Athens than the lame and the blind; which is an invincible proof that the city pleased you in a distinguishing manner, and consequently that we did, since a city never can be agreeable if its laws are not such. And yet at this time you counteract the treaty. But, if you will take our advice, Socrates, we would have you to stand to your treaty, and not expose yourself to be ridiculed by the citizens, by stealing out from hence. Pray consider what advantage can redound either to you or your friends by persisting in that goodly design. Your friends will infallibly be either exposed to danger or banished their country, or have their estates forfeited. And as for yourself, if you retire to any neighbouring city, such as Thebes or Megara, which are admirably well governed, you'll there be looked upon as an enemy. All that have any love for their country will look upon you as a corrupter of the laws. Besides, you'll fortify in them the good opinion they have of your judges, and move them to approve the sentence given against you; for a corrupter of the law will at any time pass for a debaucher of the youth, and of the vulgar people. What, will you keep out of these well-governed cities, and these assemblies of just men? But pray will you have enough to live upon in that condition? Or will you have the face to go and live with them? And pray what will you say to them, Socrates? Will you preach to them, as you did here, that virtue, justice, the laws and ordinances ought to be reverenced by men? Do you not think that this will sound very ridiculous in their ears? You ought to think so. But perhaps you'll quickly leave those well-governed cities, and go to Thessaly, to Crito's friends, where there is less order, and more licentiousness; and doubtless in that country they'll take a singular pleasure in hearing you relate in what equipage you made your escape from this prison, that is, covered with some old rags, or a beast's skin, or disguised some other way, as fugitives are wont to be. Everybody will say, 'This old fellow, that has scarce any time to live, had such a strong passion for living, that he did not stand to purchase his life by trampling under foot the most sacred laws.' Such stories will be bandied about of you at a time when you offend no man; but upon the least occasion of complaint, they'll tease you with a thousand other reproaches unworthy of you. You'll spend your time in sneaking and insinuating yourself into the favour of all men, one after another, and owning an equal subjection to them all. For what can you do? Will you feast perpetually in Thessaly, as if the good cheer had drawn you thither? But what will become then of all your fine discourses upon justice and virtue? Besides, if you design to preserve your life for the sake of your children, that cannot be in order to bring them up in Thessaly, as if you could do them no other service but make them strangers. Or if you design to leave them here, do you imagine that during your life they'll be better brought up here, in your absence, under the care of your friends? But will not your friends take the same care of them after your death that they would do in your absence? You ought to be persuaded that all those who call themselves your friends, will at all times do them all the service they can. To conclude, Socrates, submit yourself to our reasons, follow the advice of those who brought you up, and do not put your children, your life, or anything whatsoever, in the balance with justice; to the end that when you come before the tribunal of Pluto, you may be able to clear yourself before your judges. For do not deceive yourself: if you perform what you now design, you will neither better your own cause, nor that of your party ; you will neither enlarge its justice nor sanctity either here or in the regions below. But if you die bravely, you owe your death to the injustice, not of the laws, but of men ; whereas if you make your escape by repulsing so shamefully the injustice of your enemies, by violating at once both your own faith and our treaty, and injuring so many innocent persons as yourself, your friends, and your country, together with us, we will still be your enemies as long as you live; and when you are dead, our sisters, the laws in the other world, will certainly afford you no joyful reception, as knowing that you endeavoured to ruin us. Wherefore do not prefer Crito's counsel to ours."

I think, my dear Crito, I hear what I have now spoken, just as the priests of Cybele imagine they hear the cornets and flutes ; and the sound of these words makes so strong an impression in my ears, that it stops me from hearing anything else. These are the sentiments I like ; and all you can say to take me off them will be in vain. However, if you think to succeed, I do not prevent you from speaking.

Crit. I have nothing to say, Socrates.

Soc. Then be quiet, and let us courageously run this course, since God calls and guides us to it.

PHÆDO;

OR, A DIALOGUE OF THE IMMORTALITY OF THE SOUL.

PHÆDO;

OR, A DIALOGUE OF THE IMMORTALITY OF THE SOUL.

ECHECRATES and PHÆDO.

Echec. Phædo, were you present when Socrates drank the poison? Or did any one give you an account how he behaved in that juncture?

Phædo. I was present.

Echec. What were his last words then, and how expired he? You'll oblige me much with the narration; for the Philasians have but little correspondence with the Athenians, and 'tis a long time since we had any stranger from Athens to inform us how things went. We only heard that he died after drinking the poison, but could not understand any particulars concerning his death.

Phædo. What! Did you not hear how he was arraigned?

Echec. Yes, truly, somebody told us that; and we thought it strange that his sentence was so long in being put in execution after his trial.

Phædo. That happened only accidentally, for the day before his trial, the stern of the sacred ship which the Athenians send every year to Delos, was crowned for the voyage.

Echec. What is that sacred ship?

Phædo. If you credit the Athenians, it is the same ship in which Theseus transported the fourteen young children to Crete, and brought them safe back again; and 'tis said the Athenians at that time vowed to Apollo, that if the children were preserved from the impending danger, they would send every year to Delos presents and victims aboard the vessel, and this they do ever since. As soon as the ship is cleared, and ready to put to sea, they purify the city, and observe an inviolable law for putting none to death before the return of the ship. Now sometimes it stays long out, especially if the winds be contrary. This festival, which is properly called Theoria, commences when the priest of Apollo has crowned the stern of the ship. Now, as I told you, this happened on the day preceding Socrates' trial. And 'twas upon that account that he was kept so long in prison after his commitment.

Echec. And during his imprisonment, what did he do? What said he? Who was with him? Did the judges order him to be kept from visits? and did he die without the assistance of his friends?

Phœdo. Not at all : several of his friends stayed with him to the last minute.

Echec. If you're at leisure, pray relate the whole story.

Phœdo. At present I have nothing to do, and so shall endeavour to satisfy your demands. Besides, I take the greatest pleasure in the world in speaking, or hearing others speak, of Socrates.

Echec. Assure yourself, Phædo, you shall not take more pleasure in speaking than I in hearing. Begin, pray; and above all, take care to omit nothing.

Phœdo. You'll be surprised when you hear what a condition I was then in. I was so far from being sensibly touched with the misfortune of a friend whom I loved very tenderly, and who died before my eyes, that I envied his circumstances, and could not forbear to admire the goodness, sweetness, and tranquillity that appeared in all his discourses, and the bravery he showed upon the approach of death.

Everything that I saw furnishes me with a proof that he did not pass to the shades below without the assistance of some deity, that took care to conduct him, and put him in possession of that transcendent felicity of the blessed. But as, on one hand, these thoughts stifled all the sentiments of compassion that might seem due at such a mortifying sight; so, on the other hand, they lessened the pleasure I was wont to have in hearing all his other discourses, and affected me with that sorrowful reflection that, in the space of a minute, this divine man would leave us for ever. Thus was my heart crossed with contrary motions, that I could not define. 'Twas not properly either pleasure or grief, but a confused mixture of these two passions, which produced almost the same effect in all the bystanders. One while we melted into tears, and another while gave surprising signs of real joy and sensible pleasure. Above all, Apollodorus distinguished himself upon this occasion; you know his humour.

Echec. Nobody knows it better.

Phædo. In him was the difference of these motions most observable. As for me, and all the rest, our behaviour was not so distinguishing, as being mixed with the trouble and confusion I spoke of just now.

Echec. Who was there then besides yourself?

Phædo. There were no other Athenians, but Apollodorus, Critobulus, and his father Crito, Hermogenes, Epigenes, Æschines, Antisthenes, Otesippus, Menexemus, and a few more. Plato was sick.

Echec. Were there no strangers?

Phædo. Yes; Simmias the Theban, with Cebes and Phedondes; and from Megara, Euclides and Terpsion.

Echec. What! were not Aristippus and Cleombrotus there?

Phædo. No, sure; for 'tis said, they were at Ægina.

Echec. Who was there besides?

Phædo. I believe I have named most of those that were there.

Echec. Let me hear then what his last discourses were.

Phædo. I shall endeavour to give you a full account, for we never missed one day in visiting Socrates. To this end, we met every morning in the place where he was tried, which joined to the prison; and there we waited till the prison doors were opened; at which time we went straight to him, and commonly passed the whole day with him. On the day of his execution, we came thither sooner than ordinary, having heard, as we came out of the city, that the ship was returned from Delos. When we arrived, the gaoler that used to let us in came to us, and desired we would stay a little, and not go in till he came to conduct us. "For," said he, "the eleven magistrates are now untying Socrates, and acquainting him that he must die on this day." When we came in, we found Socrates untied, and his wife Xantippe (you know her) sitting by him with one of his children in her arms; and as soon as she spied us, she fell a-crying and making a noise, as you know women commonly do on such occasions. "Socrates," said she, "this is the last time your friends shall see you." Upon which Socrates, turning to Crito, said, "Crito, pray send this woman home." Accordingly 'twas done. Crito's folks carried Xantippe off, who beat her face and cried bitterly. In the meantime, Socrates, sitting upon the bed, softly strokes the place of his leg where the chain had been tied, and says, "To my mind what men call pleasure is a pretty odd sort of a thing, which agrees admirably well with pain; though people believe 'tis quite contrary, because they cannot meet in one and the same subject. For whoever enjoys the one, must unavoidably be possessed of the other, as if they were naturally joined.

"Had Æsop been aware of this truth, perhaps he had made a fable of it; and had told us that God designing to reconcile these two enemies, and not being able to compass His end, contented Himself with tying them to one chain: so that ever since the one follows the other, according to my experience at this minute. For the pain occasioned by my chain is now followed with a great deal of pleasure."

"I am infinitely glad," replies Cebes, interrupting him, " that you have mentioned Æsop, for by so doing you have put it in my head to ask you a question that many have asked me of late, especially Evenus. The question relates to your poems in turning the fables of Æsop into verse, and making a hymn to Apollo. They want to know what moved you, that never made verses before, to turn poet since you came into the prison. If Evenus asks the same question of me again, as I know he will, what would you have me to say?"

"You have nothing to do," says Socrates, "but to tell him the plain matter of fact as it stands, namely, that I did not at all mean to rival him in poetry, for I knew such an attempt was above my reach; but only to trace the meaning of some dreams, and put myself in a capacity of obeying, in case poetry happened to be the music that they allotted for my exercise. For you must know that all my lifetime I have had dreams which always recommended the same thing to me, sometimes in one form, and sometimes in another. 'Socrates,' said they, 'apply yourself to music.' This I always took for a simple exhortation, like that commonly given to those who run races, ordering me to pursue my wonted course of life, and carry on the study of wisdom, that I made my whole business, which is the most perfect music. But since my trial, the festival of Apollo having retarded the execution of my sentence, I fancied these dreams might have ordered me to apply myself to that vulgar and common sort of music: and since I was departing this world, I thought it safer to sanctify myself by obeying the gods, and essaying to make verses, than to disobey them. Pursuant to this thought, my first essay was a hymn to the god whose festival was then celebrated. After that, I considered that a true poet ought not only to make discourses in verse, but likewise fable. Now finding myself not disposed to invent new fables, I applied myself to those of Æsop, and turned those into verse that came first into my mind.

"This, my dear Cebes, is the answer you're to give Evenus; assuring him that I wish him all happiness; and tell him that if he be wise he'll follow me. For in all appearance I am to make my exit this day, since the Athenians have given orders to that effect."

"What sort of counsel is that you give to Evenus?" replies Simmias. "I have seen that man often; and by what I know of him, I can promise you, he'll never follow you with his will."

"What!" says Socrates; "is not Evenus a philosopher?"

"I think so," says Simmias.

"Then," replies Socrates, "he, and all others that are worthy of that profession, will be willing to follow me. I know he will not kill himself, for that, they say, is not lawful." Having spoken these words, he drew his legs off the bed, and sat down upon the ground, in which posture he entertained us the whole remaining part of the day.

Cebes put the first question to him, which was this: "How do you reconcile this, Socrates, that 'tis not lawful to kill one's self, and at the same time that a philosopher ought to follow you?"

"What!" replies Socrates, "did neither you nor Simmias ever hear your friend Philolaus discourse that point?"

"No," replied they; "he never explained himself clearly upon that point."

"As for me," replies Socrates, "I know nothing but what I have heard, and shall not grudge to communicate all that I have learned. Besides, there's no exercise so suitable for a man upon the point of death, as that of examining and endeavouring thoroughly to know what voyage this is that we must all make, and making known his own opinion upon it."

"What is the ground of that assertion," says Cebes, "that 'tis not lawful for a man to kill himself? I have often heard Philolaus and others say that it was an ill action, but I never heard them say more."

"Have patience," says Socrates; "you shall

know more presently, and perhaps you'll be surprised to find it an eternal truth that never changes, whereas most other things in this world alter according to their circumstances; this is still the same, even in the case of those to whom death would be more agreeable than life. Is it not a surprising thing that such men are not allowed to possess themselves of the good they want, but are obliged to wait for another deliverer?"

"Jupiter only knows that," replies Cebes, smiling.

"This may seem unreasonable to you," says Socrates, "but after all, it is not so. The discourses we are entertained with every day in our ceremonies and mysteries, viz., that God has put us in this life, as in a post which we cannot quit without His leave, etc.—these, I say, and such-like expressions, may seem hard, and surpass our understanding. But nothing is easier to be understood or better said than this, that the gods take care of men, and that men are one of the possessions that belong to the gods. Is not this true?"

"Very true," replies Cebes.

"Would not you yourself," continues Socrates, "be angry if one of your slaves killed himself without your order; and would not you punish him severely if you could?"

"Yes, doubtless," replies Cebes.

"By the same reason," says Socrates, "a man should not kill himself, but should wait for an express order from God for making his exit, like this sent me now."

"That stands to reason," says Cebes; "but your saying that a philosopher ought nevertheless to die, is what I think strange, and I cannot reconcile these two opinions, especially if it be true what you said but now, that the gods take care of men, as being their property; for that a philosopher should not be troubled to be without the gods for his guardians, and to quit a life where such perfect beings—the better governors of the world—take care of him, seems very unreasonable to me. Do they imagine they will be more capable to govern themselves when left to themselves? I can easily conceive that a fool may think it his duty to flee from a good master, at any rate; and will not be convinced that he ought to stick to what is good, and never lose sight of it. But I affirm that a wise man will desire never to quit a dependence upon a perfecter being than himself. From whence I infer the contrary of what you advanced, and conclude that the wise are sorry to die, and fools are fond of death."

Socrates seemed to be pleased with Cebes' wit; and, turning to us, told us that Cebes has always something to object, and takes care not to assent at first to what is told him.

"Indeed," replies Simmias, "I must say I find a great deal of reason in what Cebes advances. What can the sages pretend to gain by quitting better masters than themselves, and willingly depriving themselves of their aid? Do you mind that? 'Tis you alone that he addresses himself to, meaning to reprove you for your insensibility in being so willing to part with us, and quit the gods, who, according to your own words, are such good and wise governors."

"You are in the right of it," says Socrates. "I

see you mean to oblige me to make formal defences, such as I gave in at my trial."

"That's the very thing," replies Simmias.

"Then," says Socrates, "you must satisfy yourselves, so that this my last apology may have more influence upon you than my former had upon my judges. For my part," continues he, "if I thought I should not find in the other world gods as good, and as wise, and men infinitely better than we, 'twould be a piece of injustice in me not to be troubled at death. But be it known to you, Simmias, and you, Cebes, that I hope to arrive at the assembly of the just. Indeed, in this point, I may flatter myself; but as for my finding, in the other world, matters infinitely good and wise, that I can assure you of, as much as things of that nature will bear; and therefore it is that death is no trouble to me, hoping that there is something reserved for the dead after this life, and that the good meet with better treatment in the world to come than the bad."

"How!" replies Simmias, "would you have quitted this life without communicating those sentiments to us? This methinks will be a common good; and if you convince us of all that you believe with reference to this point, you have made a sufficient apology."

"That is what I design to try," says Socrates; "but I would first hear what Crito has to say. I thought he had a mind to offer something a short time ago."

"I have nothing to say," replies Crito, "but what your executioner has been pushing me on to tell you this great while, that you ought to speak as little as you can, for fear of over-heating yourself, since nothing is more contrary to the operation of poison; insomuch that, if you continue to speak so, you'll be obliged to take two or three doses."

"Let him do his office," says Socrates. "Let him make ready two doses of poison, or three if he will."

"I knew you would give me that answer," replies Crito; "but still he importunes me to speak to you."

"Pray let that alone," says Socrates, "and suffer me to explain before you, who are my judges, for what reasons a man enlightened by philosophy ought to die with courage, and a firm hope that in the other world he shall enjoy a felicity beyond anything in this. Pray do you, Simmias and Cebes, listen to my arguments.

"True philosophers make it the whole business of their lifetime to learn to die. Now, 'tis extremely ridiculous for them, after they run out a whole course incessantly in order to compass that one end, to flinch and be afraid when it comes up to them, when they are just in a capacity of obtaining it after a long and painful search."

Whereupon Simmias laughed, and told him: "In earnest, Socrates, you make me laugh, notwithstanding the small occasion I have to laugh in this juncture. For I am certain the greatest part of those who hear you talk so, will say you talk much better of the philosophers than you believe. Above all, the Athenians would be glad that all the philosophers would learn that lesson so well as to die in effect; and they'll be ready to tell you death is the only thing they are worthy of."

"Simmias," replied Socrates, "our Athenians

would so speak the truth without knowing it to be such. For they are ignorant in what manner philosophers desire to die, or how they are worthy of it. But let us leave the Athenians to themselves, and talk of things within our own company. Does death appear to be anything to you?"

"Yes, without doubt," replies Simmias.

"Is it not," continues Socrates, " the separation of soul and body ; so that the body has one separate being, and the soul another?"

"Just so," says Simmias.

"Let's try, then, my dear Simmias, if your thoughts and mine agree, by what means we shall set the object of our present inquiry in a clearer light. Do you think a philosopher courts what the world calls pleasure, as that of eating and drinking, &c.?"

"Not at all, Socrates."

"Nor that of love?"

"By no means."

"Do you think that they pursue or mind the other pleasures relating to the body, such as good clothes, handsome shoes, and the other ornaments of the body? Whether do you think they value or slight those things, when necessity does not enforce their use?"

"In my mind," replies Simmias, "a true philosopher must needs contemn them."

"Then you believe," continues Socrates, "that the body is not at all the object of the care and business of a philosopher; but, on the contrary, that his whole business is to separate himself from it, and mind only the concerns of his soul?"

"Most certainly."

"Thus," continues Socrates, "'tis plain upon the whole that a philosopher labours in a more distinguishing manner than other men to purchase the freedom of his soul, and cut off all commerce between it and the body. I am likewise of the opinion, Simmias, that most men will grant that whoever avoids those corporeal things, and takes no pleasure in them, is not worthy to live; and that he who does not use the pleasures of the body is near to death."

"You speak truth, Socrates.'

"But what shall we say of the acquiring of prudence? Is the body an obstacle or not, when employed in that work? I'll explain my meaning by an example: Have seeing and hearing anything of truth in them, and is their testimony faithful? Or are the poets in the right in singing that we neither see nor hear things truly? For, if these two senses of seeing and hearing are not true and trusty, the others which are much weaker, will be far less such. Do not you think so?"

"Yes, without doubt," replies Simmias.

"When does the soul, then," continues Socrates, "find out the truth? We see that while the body is joined in the inquiry, this body plainly cheats and seduces it."

"That is true," says Simmias.

"Is it not by reasoning that the soul embraces truth? And does it not reason better than before, when 'tis not encumbered by seeing or hearing, pain or pleasure? When shut up within itself, it bids adieu to the body, and entertains as little correspondence with it as possible, and pursues the knowledge of things without touching them."

"That is incomparably well spoken."

"Is it not, especially upon this occasion, that the soul of a philosopher despises and avoids the body, and wants to be by itself?"

"I think so."

"What shall we say, then, my dear Simmias, of all the objects of the soul? For instance, shall we call justice something or nothing?"

"We must certainly give it the title of Something."

"Shall we not likewise call it Good and Fine?"

"Ay, doubtless."

"But did you ever see these objects with the eye of your body? Or with any other sense? Did you ever touch any of those things I now speak of, such as magnitude, health, fortitude, and, in a word, the essence of all other things? Is the truth of them discovered by the body? Or is it not certain that whoever puts himself in a condition to examine them more narrowly, and trace them to the bottom, will better compass the end, and know more of them?"

"That's very true."

"Now the simplest and purest way of examining

things is to pursue every particular thought alone, without offering to support our meditation by seeing, or backing our reasonings by any other corporeal sense; by employing the naked thought without any mixture, and so endeavouring to trace the pure and genuine essence of things without the ministry of the eyes or ears : the soul being, if I may so speak, entirely disengaged from the whole mass of body, which only cumbers the soul, and cramps it in the quest of wisdom and truth, as often as it is admitted to the least correspondence with it. If the essence of things be ever known, must it not be in the manner above mentioned ?"

"Right, Socrates : you have spoke incomparably well."

"Is it not a necessary consequence from this principle," continues Socrates, "that true philosophers should have such language among themselves? This life is a road that's apt to mislead us and our reason in our inquiries, because, while we have a body, and while our soul is drowned in so much corruption, we shall never attain the object of our wishes, *i.e.*, truth. The body throws a thousand obstacles and crosses in our way, by demanding necessary food; and then the diseases that ensue do quite disorder our inquiry. Besides, it fills us with love, desires, fears, and a thousand foolish imaginations, insomuch that there is nothing truer than the common saying, 'That the body will never conduct us to wisdom.' What is it that gives rise to wars, and occasions seditions and duelling? Is it not the body and its desires? In effect, all wars take rise from the desire of riches, which we are forced to heap up for the sake of our body, in order to supply its wants, and serve it like slaves. 'Tis this that cramps our application to philosophy. And the greatest of all our evils is that when it has given us some respite, and we are set upon meditation, it steals in and interrupts our meditation all of a sudden. It cumbers, troubles, and surprises us in such a manner that it hinders us from descrying the truth. Now we have made it out, that in order to trace the purity and truth of anything, we should lay aside the body, and only employ the soul to examine the objects we pursue. So that we can never arrive at the wisdom we court till after death. Reason is on our side. For if it is impossible to know anything purely while we are in the body, one of these two things must be true: either the truth is never known, or it is known after death; because at that time the soul will be left to itself, and freed of its burden, and not before. And while we are in this life, we can only approach to the truth in proportion to our removing from the body, and renouncing all correspondence with it that is not of mere necessity, and keeping ourselves clear from the contagion of its natural corruption, and all its filth, till God Himself comes to deliver us. Then, indeed, being freed from all bodily folly, we shall converse, in all probability, with men that enjoy the same liberty, and shall know within ourselves the pure essence of things, which perhaps is nothing but the truth. But he who is not pure is not allowed to approach to purity itself. This, my dear Simmias, as I take it, should be the thought and language of true philosophers. Are not you of the same mind?"

"Most certainly, Socrates.

"Then, my dear Simmias, whoever shall arrive

where I am now going, has great reason to hope that he will there be possessed of what we look for here with so much care and anxiety; so that the voyage I am now sent upon fills me with a sweet and agreeable hope. And it will have the same effect upon all who are persuaded that the soul must be purged before it knows the truth. Now the purgation of the soul, as we were saying but just now, is only its separation from the body, its accustoming itself to retire and lock itself up, renouncing all commerce with it as much as possible, and living by itself, whether in this or the other world, without being chained to the body."

"All that is true, Socrates."

"Well! what we call death, is not that the disengagement and separation of the body from the soul?"

"Most certainly."

"Are not the true philosophers the only men that seek after this disengagement? and is not that separation and deliverance their whole business?"

"So I think, Socrates."

"Is it not a ridiculous fancy, that a man that

has lived in the expectation of death, and during his whole lifetime has been preparing to die, upon his arrival at the point of desired death, should think to retire, and be afraid of it. Would not that be a very scandalous apostasy?"

" How should it be otherwise?"

"'Tis certain, then, Simmias, that death is so far from being terrible to true philosophers that 'tis their whole business to die; which may be easily inferred thus: if they slight and contemn their body, and passionately desire to enjoy their soul by itself, is it not a piece of extravagance to decline going to that place, where those who get to it, hope to obtain the good things they have wished for all their lifetime? For they desired wisdom, and a deliverance from the body, as being their burden, and the object of their hatred and contempt. Do not many upon the loss of their mistresses, wives, or children, willingly cut the thread of life, and convey themselves into the other world, merely upon the hope of meeting there, and cohabiting with the persons they love? And shall a true lover of wisdom, and one that firmly hopes to attain the perfection of it in the other world, shall he be startled by death, and be unwilling to go to the place that will furnish him with what his soul loves? Doubtless, my dear Simmias, if he be a true philosopher, he'll go with a great deal of pleasure; as being persuaded that there's no place in the regions below that can furnish him with that pure wisdom that he's in quest of. Now, if things stand thus, would it not be a piece of extravagance in such a man to fear death?"

"To be sure," says Simmias, "it would be so with a witness."

"And consequently," continues Socrates, "when a man shrinks and retires at the point of death, it is a certain evidence that he loves not wisdom, but his own body, or honour, or riches, or perhaps all three together."

"'Tis so, Socrates."

"Then, Simmias, does not what we call Fortitude belong in a peculiar manner to philosophers? And does not Temperance, or that sort of wisdom that consists in controlling our desires, and living soberly and modestly, suit admirably well with those who contemn their bodies, and live philosophically?"

"That is certain, Socrates."

"Were you to inspect the fortitude and temperance of other men, you'll find 'em very ridiculous."

"How so, Socrates?"

"You know," says he, "all other men look upon death as the greatest affliction."

"That's true," replies Simmias.

"When those you call stout suffer death with some courage, they do it only for fear of some greater evil."

"That I must grant."

"And by consequence, all men, barring the philosophers, are only stout and valiant through fear. And is it not ridiculous to believe a man to be brave and valiant that is only influenced by fear and timorousness?"

"You are in the right, Socrates."

"Is not the case the same with your temperate persons? 'Tis only intemperance makes them such. Though at first view this may seem impossible, yet it is no more than what daily experience shows to be the result of that foolish and ridiculous temperance. For such persons disclaim one pleasure only for fear of being robbed of other pleasures that they covet, and which have an ascendant over them. They'll cry out to you as long as you will, that intemperance consists in being ruled and over-awed by our passions; but at the same time that they give you this fine definition, 'tis only their subjection to some predominant pleasures that make them discard others. Now this is much what I have just said, that they are only temperate through intemperance."

"That is very clear, Socrates."

"Let us not be imposed upon, my dear Simmias: the straight road to virtue does not lie in shifting pleasures for pleasures, fears for fears, or one melancholy thought for another, and imitating those who change a large piece of money for many small ones. But wisdom is the only true and unalloyed coin, for which all others must be given in exchange. With that piece of money we purchase all fortitude, temperance, justice. In a word, that virtue is always true that accompanies wisdom, without any dependence upon pleasures, grief, fears, or any other passions. Whereas all other virtues stripped of wisdom, which run upon a perpetual exchange, are only shadows of virtue. True virtue is really and in effect a purgation from all these sorts of passions. Temperance, justice, fortitude, and prudence, or wisdom itself, are not exchanged for passions, but cleanse us of them. And it is pretty evident, that those who instituted the purifications called by us Teletes, *i.e.*, perfect expiations, were persons of no contemptible rank, men of great genius, who in the first ages meant by such riddles to give us to know that whoever enters the other world without being initiated and purified shall be hurled headlong into the vast abyss; and that whoever arrives there after due purgation and expiation shall be lodged in the apartment of the gods. For, as the dispensers of these expiations say, 'There are many who bear the Thyrsus, but few that are possessed by the spirit of God.' Now those who are thus possessed, as I take it, are the true philosophers. I have tried all means to be lifted in that number, and have made it the business of my whole life to compass my end. If it please God, I hope to know in a minute that my efforts have not been ineffectual, and that success has crowned my endeavours. This, my dear Simmias, and my dear Cebes, is the apology with which I offer to justify my not [being troubled or afflicted for parting with you, and quitting my governors in this life; hoping to find good friends and rulers there, as well as here. This the vulgar cannot digest. However, I shall be satisfied if my defences take better with you than they did with my judges."

Socrates having thus spoken, Cebes took up the discourse to this purpose. "Socrates, I subscribe to the truth of all you have said, There is only one thing that men look upon as incredible, viz., what you advanced of the soul. For almost everybody fancies that when the soul parts from the body it is no more, it dies along with it; in the very minute of parting it vanishes, like a vapour or smoke which flies off, and disperses, and has no existence. For if it subsisted by itself, were gathered and retired into itself, and freed from all the above-mentioned evils, there were a fair and promising prospect ascertaining the truth of what you have said. But, that the soul lives after the death of a man, that it is sensible, that it acts and thinks, that, I say, needs both insinuation and solid proofs to make it go down."

"You say right, Cebes," replies Socrates, "but how shall we manage the affair? Shall we in this interview examine whether that is probable or not?"

"I shall be very glad," says Cebes, "to hear your thoughts upon the matter."

"At least," says Socrates, "I cannot think that any man hearing us, though he were a comedian, would upbraid me with raillery, and charge me with not speaking of such things as concern us very much. If you have a mind that we should trace this affair to the bottom, my opinion is that we should proceed in the following method, in order to know whether the souls of the dead have a being in the other world or not.

"'Tis a very ancient opinion, that souls quitting this world repair to the infernal regions, and return after that to live in the world. If it be so, that men return to life after death, it follows necessarily that during that interval their souls are lodged in the lower regions; for if they had not a being they could not return to this world. For this will be a sufficient proof of what we affirm, if we be convinced that the living spring from the dead: if otherwise, then we must look out for other proofs."

"That is certain," says Cebes.

"But to assure ourselves of this truth," replies Socrates, "'tis not sufficient to examine the point upon the comparison with men : but likewise upon that with other animals, plants, and whatever has a vegetable principle. By that means we shall be convinced that all things are born after the same manner—that is, whatever has a contrary—owes its first rise to its contrary. For instance, handsome is the contrary to ugly, and just to unjust. And the same is the case of an infinite number of other things. Now, let's see if it be absolutely necessary that whatever has a contrary should spring from that contrary. As when a thing becomes bigger, of necessity it must formerly have been lesser before it acquired that magnitude. And when it dwindles into a lesser form, it must needs have been greater before its diminution. In like manner the strongest arises from the weakest, and the swiftest from the slowest."

"That's a plain truth," says Cebes.

"And pray," continues Socrates, "when a thing becomes worse, was it not formerly better? and when it grows just, is it not because it was formerly more unjust?"

"Yes, surely, Socrates."

"Then it is sufficiently proved that everything is generated by its contrary."

"Sufficiently, Socrates."

"But is not there always a certain medium between these two contraries? There are two births, or two processions, one of this from that, and another of that from this. The medium between a greater and a lesser thing is increase and diminution. The same is the case of what we call mixing, separating, heating, cooling, and all other things *in infinitum*. For though it sometimes falls out that we have not terms to express those changes and mediums, yet experience shows that by an absolute necessity things take rise from one another, and pass reciprocally from one to another through a medium.

"There's no doubt of that."

"And what," continues Socrates, "has not life likewise its contrary, as awaking has sleeping?"

"Without doubt," says Cebes.

"What is the contrary?"

"Death."

"Since these two things are contrary, do not they take rise one from the other? And between these two are there not two generations, or two processions?

"Why not?"

"But," says Socrates, "I am about to tell you how the new-mentioned combination stands, and to show you the origin and progress of each of these two things which make up the compound. Pray tell [me how awaking and sleeping are related? Does not sleep beget watchfulness and watching sleep? And is not the generation of sleep the falling asleep? and that of watching the awaking?

"All very clear."

"Now, pray view the combination of life and death. Is not death the contrary of life?

"Yes."

"And does not the one breed the other?"

"Yes."

"What is it that life breeds?"

"Death."

"What is it that death breeds?"

"It must certainly be life."

"Then," says Socrates, "all living things and men are bred from death."

"So I think," says Cebes.

"And, by consequence," continues Socrates, "our souls are lodged in the infernal world after our death."

"The consequence seems just."

"But of these two generations, one, viz., death, is very palpable: it discovers itself to the eye, and is touched by the hand."

"Most certainly."

"Shall we not then attribute to death the virtue of producing its contrary, as well as to life? Or shall we say that nature is lame and maimed on that score?"

"There's an absolute necessity," replies Cebes, " of ascribing to death the generation of its contrary."

"What is that contrary?

"Reviving, or returning to life."

"If there is such a thing as returning to life, 'tis nothing else but the birth of the dead returning to life. And thus we agree that the living are as much the product of the dead, as the dead are of the living. Which is an incontestable proof that the souls of the dead must remain in some place or other, from whence they return to life."

" That, as I take it, Cebes, is a necessary consequence from the principles we have agreed on.

" And, as I take it, Cebes, these principles are well grounded. Consider them yourself. If all these contraries had not their productions and generations in their turns, which make a circle; and if there were nothing but one birth, and one direct product from one to the other contrary, without the return of the last contrary to the first that produce it; were it not so, all things would terminate in the same figure, and be affected in the same manner, and at last cease to be born."

"How do you say, Socrates?"

"There's no difficulty in conceiving what I now say. If there was nothing but sleep, and if sleep did not produce watching, 'tis plain that everything would be an emblem of the fable of Endymion, and nothing would be seen anywhere, because the same thing must happen to them which happened to Endymion, viz., they must always sleep. If everything were mingled without any subsequent separation, we should quickly see Anaxagoras's doctrine fulfilled, and all things jumbled together. At the same rate, my dear Cebes, if all living things died, and being dead, continued such without reviving, would not all things unavoidably come to an end at last, insomuch that there would not be a living thing left in being? For if living things did not arise from dead ones when the living ones die, of necessity all things must at last be swallowed up by death, and entirely annihilated."

"It is necessarily so," replies Cebes; "all that you have said seems to be incontestable."

"As I take it, Cebes, there is no objection made against those truths, neither are we mistaken in receiving them; for 'tis certain there is a return to life; 'tis certain that the living rise out of the dead; that the souls departed have a being, and upon their returning to this life, the good souls are in a better, and the bad ones in a worse condition."

"What you now advance," says Cebes, interrupting Socrates, "is only a necessary consequence of another principle that I have often heard you lay down, viz., that all our acquired knowledge is only remembrance. For if that principle be true, we must necessarily have learnt at another time what we call to mind in this. Now that's impossible, unless our soul had a being before its being invested with this human form. So that this same principle concludes the immortality of the soul."

"But, Cebes," says Simmias, interrupting him, "what demonstration have we of that principle? Pray refresh my memory with it, for at present it is out of my head."

"There's a very pretty demonstration for it, replies Cebes: "all men being duly interrogated, find out all things of themselves, which they could never do without knowledge and right reason. Put them at unawares upon the figure of geometry, and other things of that nature, they'll presently perceive that 'tis as 'tis said."

"Simmias," says Socrates, "if you will not rely upon this experience, pray try, whether the same method will not bring you over to our sentiments. Do you find great difficulty in believing that learning is only remembering?"

"I do not find very much," replies Simmias; "but I would gladly learn that remembrance you speak of. By what Cebes has said, I almost remember it, and I begin to believe it; but that shall not hinder me from hearing with pleasure the arguments you can offer for it."

"I argue thus," replies Socrates: "We all agree, that in order to remember, a man must have known before what he then calls to mind."

"Most certainly."

"And let us likewise agree upon this, that knowledge coming in a certain manner is remembrance. I say, in a certain manner : for instance, when a man by feeling, hearing, or perceiving a thing by any of the senses knows what it is that thus strikes the senses, and at the same time imagines to himself another thing, independent of that knowledge, by virtue of a quite different knowledge, do not we justly say that the man remembers the thing that comes thus into his mind ? "

" How do you say ? " replies Simmias.

" I say," replies Socrates, " for example, that we know a man by one sort of knowledge, and a harp by another."

" That's certain," quoth Simmias.

" Well, then," continues Socrates, " do not you know what happens to lovers, when they see the harp, habit, or any other thing, that their friends or mistresses used to make use of ? It is just as I said but now. Upon seeing and knowing the harp they form in their thoughts the image of the person to whom the harp belongs. This is remembrance. Thus it often falls out that one seeing Simmias, thinks of Cebes. I could cite a thousand instances.

This, then, is remembrance, especially when the things called to mind are such as had been forgot through length of time, or being out of sight."

"That is very certain," quoth Simmias.

"But," continues Socrates, "upon seeing the picture of a horse or harp, may not one call to mind the man? and upon seeing the picture of Simmias, may not one think of Cebes?"

"Sure enough," says Simmias.

"Much more," continues Socrates, "upon seeing the picture of Simmias, will he call to mind Simmias himself?"

"Ay, with ease."

"From all these instances we infer that remembrance is occasioned sometimes by things that are like the thing remembered, and sometimes by things that are unlike. But when one remembers a thing by virtue of a likeness, does it not necessarily come to pass that the mind at first view discovers whether the picture does resemble the thing designed lamely or perfectly?"

"It must needs be so," replies Simmias.

"Then pray mind whether your thoughts of

what I am about to say agree with mine. Is not there something that we call equality? I do not speak of the equality between one tree and another, one stone and another, and several other things that are alike: I speak of the abstracted equality of things. Shall we call that something or nothing?"

"Surely, we must call it something; but that will only come to pass when we mean to speak philosophically and of marvellous things."

"But then do we know this equality?"

"Without doubt."

"From whence do we derive that knowledge? Is it not from the things we mentioned but now? 'Tis upon seeing equal trees, equal stones, and several other things of the nature, that we form the idea of that equality, which is not either the trees or the stones, but something abstracted from all subjects. Do not you find it such? Pray take notice. The stones and the trees are always the same, and yet do not they sometimes appear unequal?"

"Sure enough."

"What! Do equal things appear unequal? Or, does equality take up the form of inequality?"

"By no means, Socrates."

"Then equality, and the thing which is equal, are two different things?"

"Most certainly."

"But after all, these equal things, which are different from equality, furnish us with the idea and knowledge of that abstracted equality."

"That's true," replies Simmias.

"The case is the same, whether this equality bears a resemblance to the things that occasioned its idea or not."

"Most certainly."

"When, upon seeing one thing, you call to mind another, 'tis no matter if it be like it or not; still it is remembrance."

"Without doubt."

"But what shall we say to this," continues Socrates, "when we behold trees or other things that are equal, are they equal according to the idea or not?"

"Very far from it."

"Then we agree upon this. When a man sees a thing before him, and thinks it would be equal to another thing, but at the same time is far from being so perfectly equal as the equality of which he has the idea, then, I say, he who thinks thus must necessarily have known beforehand this intellectual being which the thing resembles, but imperfectly."

"There's an absolute necessity for that."

"And is not the case the same when we compare things equal with the equality?"

"Sure enough, Socrates."

"Then of necessity we must have known that equality before the time in which we saw the equal things, and thereupon thought that they all tender to be equal as equality itself, but could not reach it."

"That is certain."

"But we likewise agree upon this, that this thought can be derived from nothing else but one of our senses, from seeing, touching, or feeling one way or other. And the same conclusion will hold of all things, whether intellectual or sensible."

"All things will equally conclude for what you design."

"Then 'tis from the senses themselves that we derive this thought; that all the objects of our senses have a tendency towards this intellectual equality, but come short of it. Is it not?"

"Yes, without doubt, Socrates."

"In effect, Simmias, before we began to see, feel, or use our senses, we must have had the knowledge of this intellectual equality, else we could not be capable to compare it with the sensible things, and perceive that they have all a tendency towards it, but fall short of its perfection."

"That is a necessary consequence from the premises."

"But it is not certain, that immediately after our birth we saw, we heard, and made use of our other senses?"

"Very true."

"Then it follows, that before that time we had the knowledge of that equality?"

"Without doubt."

"And by consequence we were possessed of it before we were born."

"So I think."

"If we possessed it before we were born, then we knew things before we were born, and immediately after our birth; knew not only what is equal, what great, what small, but all other things of that nature. For what we now advance of equality is equally applicable to goodness, justice, sanctity, and, in a word, to all other things that have a real existence. So that of necessity we must have known all these things before we came into this world."

"That's certain."

"And being possessed of that knowledge, if we did not forget apace every day, we should not only be born with it, but retain it all our lifetime. For to know is only to preserve the knowledge we have received, and to lose it. And to forget is to lose the knowledge we enjoy before."

"That's certain, Socrates."

"Now if, after having possessed that knowledge before we were born, and having lost it since, we come to retrieve it by the ministry of our senses which we call learning, shall we not justly entitle it Remembrance?"

"With a great deal of reason, Socrates."

"For we have agreed upon this, that 'tis very possible that a man seeing, hearing, or perceiving one thing by any one of his senses, should frame to himself the imagination of another thing that he had forgot; to which the thing perceived by the senses has some relation, whether it resembles the other or not. So that one of two things must necessarily follow; either we were born with that knowledge, and preserved it all along, or else retrieved it afterwards by way of remembrance. Which of these two do you pitch upon, Simmias? Are we born with that knowledge, or do we call it to mind after having had it, and forgot it?"

"Indeed, Socrates, I do not know which to choose at present."

"But mind what I am about to say to you, and then let us see which you'll choose. A man that knows anything, can he give a reason for his knowledge or not?"

"Doubtless he can, Socrates."

"And you think all men can give a reason for what we have been speaking of ?"

"I wish they could," replies Simmias; "but I'm afraid to-morrow we shall have none here that's capable to do it."

"Then you think all men have not this knowledge ?"

"No, surely."

"Do they call to mind, then, the things they have known ?"

"That may be."

"At what time did our souls learn that knowledge ? It cannot be since we were men."

"No, surely."

"Then it must be some time before that."

"Yes, without doubt."

"And, by consequence, Simmias, our souls had a being before that time, that is to say, before they were invested with a human form, while they knew and understood."

"Unless you'll allow, Socrates, that we learned it in the minute of our birth. There is no other time left."

"Be it so, my dear Simmias, but at what other time did we lose it? For we did not bring it into the world with us, as we concluded but now. Did we lose it in the same minute that we obtained it? Or can you assign any other time?"

"No, Socrates, I did not perceive that what I said was to no purpose."

"Then, Simmias, this must be a standing truth. That if the objects of our daily conversation have a real existence, I mean, if justice, goodness, and all that essence with which we compare the objects of our senses, and which having an existence before us, proves to be of the same nature with our own essence, and is the standard by which we measure all things. I say, if all these things have a real existence, our soul is likewise entitled to existence, and that before we were born; and if these things have no being, then all our discourses are useless. Is it not a standing truth, and withal a just and necessary consequence, that the existence of our souls before our birth stands and falls with that of those things?"

"That consequence," replies Simmias, "seems to

me to be equally just and wonderful, and the result of the whole discourse affords something very glorious and desirable on our behalf, since it concludes that before we were born our souls had an existence, as well as that intelligible essence you mentioned but now. For my part, I think there's nothing more evident, and more sensible, than the existence of all these things, goodness, justice, &c., and you have sufficiently made it out."

"Now for Cebes," says Socrates; "for Cebes must likewise be convinced."

"I believe," replies Simmias, "though he is the stiffest man upon earth, and very much proof against arguments, yet he'll own your proof to be very convincing. In the meantime, though I am sufficiently convinced that our souls had a being before we were born, I have not yet heard sufficient proof for its continuing after our death. For that popular opinion, which Cebes mentioned but now, remains in all its force, viz., that after the death of men the soul disperses and ceases to be. And indeed I cannot see why the soul should not be born, or proceed from some part or other, and have a being before it animates the body in this life; and when it removes from the body, ceases to be, and makes its exit as well as the body."

"You speak well, Simmias," says Cebes; "to my mind, Socrates has only proved the half of what he proposed. 'Tis true he demonstrated that the soul has a being before the body; but to complete his demonstration he should have proved that our soul has an existence after death, as well as before this life."

"But I have demonstrated it to you both," replies Socrates; "and you'll be sensible of it, if you join this last proof with what you acknowledge before, viz., that the living rise from the dead. For if 'tis true that our soul was in being before we were born, then, of necessity, when it comes to life it proceeds, so to speak, from the bosom of death; and why should it not lie under the same necessity of being after death, since it must return to life? Thus, what you speak of is made out. But I perceive both of you desire to sound this matter to the bottom; and are apprehensive, like children, that when the soul departs the body the winds run away with it, and disperses it, especially when a man dies in an open country, in a place exposed to the winds."

Whereupon Cebes, smiling, replied, "Pray, then, Socrates, try to discuss our fears, or rather convince us, as if we feared nothing. Though, indeed, there be some among us who lie under those childish apprehensions. Persuade us, then, not to fear death as a vain phantom."

"As for that," says Socrates, "you must employ spells and exorcisms every day till you be cured."

"But pray, Socrates, where shall we meet with an excellent conjurer, since you are going to leave us?"

"Greece is large enough," replies Socrates, "and well stored with learned men. Besides, there are a great many barbarous nations which you must scour in order to find out the conjurer, without sparing either labour or charges, for you cannot employ your money in a better cause. You must likewise look for one among yourselves, for 'tis possible there may be none found more capable to perform those enchantments than yourselves."

"We shall obey your order, Socrates, in looking out for one; but in the meanwhile, if you please, let us resume our former discourse."

"With all my heart, Cebes."

"Well said, Socrates."

"The first question we ought to ask ourselves," says Socrates, "is, What sort of things they are that are apt to be dissipated, what things are liable to that accident, and what part of those things? Then we must inquire into the nature of the soul, and form our hopes or fears accordingly."

"That's very true."

"Is it not certain, that only compounded things, or such as are of a compoundable nature, admit of being dissipated at the same rate that they were compounded? If there are any uncompounded beings, they alone are free from this accident, and naturally incapable of dissipation."

"That, I think, is very clear," replies Cebes.

"Is it not very likely that things which are

always the same, and in the same condition, are not at all compounded? and that those which are liable to perpetual changes, and are never the same, are certainly compounded."

"I am of your mind, Socrates."

"Let us betake ourselves to the things we were speaking of but now, the existence whereof is never contested either in question or answer. Are these always the same, or do they sometimes change? Equality, beauty, goodness, and every singular thing—*i.e.*, the essence itself—do these receive the least alteration, or are they so pure and simple that they continue always the same, without undergoing the least change?"

"Of necessity," replies Cebes, "they must continue still the same without alteration."

"And all these fine things," says Socrates, "such as men, horses, habits, movables, and a great many other things of the same nature, are they entirely opposite to the former, that they never continue in the same condition, either with reference to themselves or others, but are subject to perpetual alterations?"

"They never continue in the same condition," replies Cebes.

"Now these are the things that are visible, touchable, perceptible by some other sense; whereas the former, which continue still the same, can only be reached by thought, as being immaterial and invisible."

"That's true, Socrates."

"If you please," continues Socrates, "I'll instance in two things—the one visible, the other invisible; one still the same, and the other betraying continual alterations."

"With all my heart," says Cebes.

"Let us see, then. Are not we compounded of a body and a soul; or is there any other ingredient in our composition?"

"No, surely."

"Which of the two kinds of things does our body most resemble?"

"All men own that it is most conformable to the visible sort."

"And pray, my dear Cebes, is our soul visible or invisible?"

OF THE IMMORTALITY OF THE SOUL. 97

"At least 'tis not visible to men."

"But when we speak of visible or invisible things, we mean with reference to men, without minding any other nature. Once more, then, is the soul visible or not?"

"'Tis not visible."

"Then 'tis immaterial and invisible?"

"Yes."

"And by consequence the soul is more conformable than the body to the invisible kind of things, and the body suits better with the visible?"

"There is an absolute necessity for that."

"When the soul makes use of the body in considering anything, by seeing, hearing, or any other sense (that being the sole function of the body, to consider things by the senses), should not we then say that the body draws the soul upon mutable things? In this condition it strays, frets, staggers, and is giddy like a man in drink, by reason of its being engaged in matter. Whereas, when it pursues things by itself without calling in the body, it betakes itself to what is pure, immortal,

p - 125

immutable; and as being of the same nature, dwells constantly upon it while it is master of itself. Then its errors are at an end, and it is always the same, as being united to what never changes; and this passion of the soul is what we call wisdom or prudence."

"That's admirably well spoken, Socrates, and a very great truth."

"After all, then, what sort of things does the soul seem to resemble most?"

"To my mind, Socrates, there is no man so stupid and stiff as not to be obliged, by your method of arguing, to acknowledge that the soul bears a greater resemblance and conformity to the immutable being, than to that which is always upon the change."

"And as for the body?"

"It bears a greater resemblance to the other."

"Let's try another way. During the conjunction of body and soul, nature orders the one to obey and be a slave, and the other to command and hold the empire. Which of these two characters is most suitable to the Divine Being, and which to that is mortal? Are not you sensible that the divine is only capable of commanding and ruling, and what mortal is only worthy of obedience and slavery?"

"Sure enough."

"Which of these two, then, agrees best with the soul?"

"'Tis evident, Socrates, that our soul resembles what is divine, and our body what is mortal."

"You see, then, my dear Cebes, the necessary result of all is, that our soul bears a strict resemblance to what is divine, immortal, intellectual, simple, indissolvable; and is always the same, and always like, and that our body does perfectly resemble what is human, mortal, sensible, compounded, dissolvable, always changing, and never like itself. Can anything be alleged to destroy that consequence or to make out the contrary?"

"No, surely, Socrates."

"Does not it, then, suit with the body to be quickly dissolved, and with the soul to be always indissolvable, or something very near it?"

"That is a standing truth."

"Accordingly you see every day, when a man dies, his visible body, that continues exposed to our view, and which we call the corpse, that alone admits of dissolution, alteration, and dissipation: this, I say, does not immediately undergo any of these accidents, but continues a pretty while in its entire form, or in its flower, if I may so speak, especially in this season. Bodies embalmed after the manner of those in Egypt remain entire for an infinity of years, and even in those that corrupt, there are always some parts, such as the bones, nerves, and the like, that continue in a manner immortal. Is not this true?"

"Very true."

"Now as for the soul, which is an invisible being, that goes to a place like itself, marvellous, pure, and invisible, in the infernal world; and returns to a God full of goodness and wisdom, which I hope will be the fate of my soul in a minute, if it please God. Shall a soul of this nature, and created with all these advantages, be dissipated and annihilated, as soon as it parts from the body, as most men believe? No such thing, my dear

Simmias, and my dear Cebes. I'll tell you what will rather come to pass, and what we ought to believe steadily. If the soul retain its purity without any mixture of filth from the body, as having entertained no voluntary correspondence with it, but on the contrary, having always avoided it, and recollected itself within itself in continual meditations; that is, in studying the true philosophy, and effectually learning to die; for philosophy is a preparation to death : I say, if the soul departs in this condition, it repairs to a being like itself, a being that's divine, immortal, and full of wisdom; in which it enjoys an inexpressible felicity, as being freed from its errors, its ignorance, its fears, its amours, that tyrannised over it, and all the other evils pertaining to human nature : and as 'tis said of those who have been initiated into holy mysteries, it truly passes a whole course of eternity with the gods? Ought not this to be the matter of our belief?"

" Sure enough, Socrates."

" But if the soul depart full of uncleanness and impurity, as having been all along mingled with the body, always employed in its service, always possessed by the love of it, wheedled and charmed by its pleasures and lusts, insomuch that it is believed there was nothing real or true beyond what is corporeal, what may be seen, touched, drank, or eaten, or what is the object of carnal pleasures, that it hated, dreaded, and avoided what the eyes of the body could not descry, and all that is intelligible, and can only be enjoyed by philosophy. Do you think, I say, that a soul in this condition can depart pure and simple from the body?"

"No, surely, Socrates, that's impossible."

"On the contrary, it departs stained with corporeal pollution, which was rendered natural to it by its continual commerce and too intimate union with the body, at a time when it was its constant companion, and was still employed in serving and gratifying it."

"Most certainly."

"This pollution, my dear Cebes, is a gross, heavy, earthy, and visible mass; and the soul loaded with such a weight, is dragged into that visible place, not only by the weight, but by its own dreading the light and the invisible place; and, as we commonly say, it wanders in the churchyards, round the tombs, where dark phantoms and apparitions are often seen, such as these souls that did not depart the body in purity or simplicity, but polluted with that earthy and visible matter that makes them degenerate into a visible form."

"That is very likely, Socrates."

"Yes without doubt, Cebes; and 'tis also likely that 'tis not the good but the bad souls that are forced to wander in those places of impurity, where they suffer for their former ill-life, and continue to wander, till through the love they have to this corporeal mass, which always follows them, they engage again in a new body, and in all probability plunge themselves into the same manners and passions as were the occupation of the first life."

"How do you say, Socrates?"

"I say, Cebes, that for instance those who made their belly their god, and loved nothing but indolence and impurity, without any shame, and without any reserve; those enter into the bodies of asses or such like creatures. Do not you think this very probable?"

"Yes, surely, Socrates."

"And those souls which loved only injustice, tyranny, and rapine, are employed to animate the bodies of wolves, hawks, and falcons. Where else should souls of that stamp go?"

"Nowhere else, Socrates."

"The case of all the rest is much the same. They go to animate the bodies of beasts of different species, according as they resemble their first courses."

"According to these principles, it cannot be otherwise."

"The happiest of all these men, whose souls are sent to the most agreeable place, are those who have always made a profession of popular and civil virtues, which are called temperance and justice, to which they have brought themselves only by habit and exercise, without any assistance from philosophy and the mind."

"How can they be so happy, then?"

"'Tis probable that after their death their souls are joined to the bodies of politic and meek animals, such as bees, wasps, and ants; or else return to human bodies, and become temperate and wise men. But as for approaching to the nature of God, that is not at all allowed to those who did not live philosophically, and whose souls did not depart with all their purity. The great privilege is reserved for the love of true wisdom. And 'tis upon the consideration of this, my dear Simmias, and my dear Cebes, that the true philosophers renounce the desires of the body, and keep themselves up from its lusts; they are not apprehensive of the ruin of their families, or of poverty, as the vulgar are, and those who are wedded to their riches: they fear neither ignominy nor reproach, as those do who court only dignities and honour. In a word, they renounce all things and even themselves."

"It would not be suitable for them to do otherwise," replies Cebes.

"No, surely," continues Socrates. "In the like manner, all those who value their souls, and do not live for the body, depart from all such lusts, and follow a different course from those insensible creatures that do not know where they go. They are persuaded that they ought not to do anything contrary to philosophy, or harbour anything that destroys its purifications and retards their liberty; and accordingly resign themselves to its conduct, and follow it whithersoever it leads them."

"How do you say, Socrates?"

"I'll explain it to you. The philosophers, finding their soul tied and chained to the body, and by that means obliged to employ the body in the pursuit of objects which it cannot follow alone, so that it still floats in an abyss of ignorance, are very sensible that the force of this bond lies in its own desires, insomuch that the prisoner itself helps to lock up the chains. They are sensible that philosophy, coming to seize upon the soul in this condition, gently instructs and comforts it, and endeavours to disengage it, by giving it to know that the eye of the body is full of illusion and deceit, as well as all its other senses, by advertising it not to use the body farther than necessity requires; and advising it to recollect and shut up itself within itself; to receive no disposition but its own after it has examined within itself the intrinsic nature of every thing, and stripped it of the covering that conceals it from our eyes, and to continue fully persuaded that whatever is tried by all its other senses, being different from the former discovery, is certainly false; now whatever is tried by the corporeal senses is visible. And what it views by itself without the ministry of the body is invisible and unintelligible. So that the soul of a true philosopher, being convinced that it should not oppose its own liberty, disclaims as far as is possible the pleasures, lusts, fears, and sorrows of the body: for it knows that when one has enjoyed many pleasures or given way to extreme grief or timorousness, or given himself to his desires, he not only is afflicted by the sensible evils known to all the world, such as the loss of health or estate, but is doomed to the last and greatest of evils—an evil that is so much the more dangerous and terrible that it is not obvious to our senses."

"What evil is that, Socrates?"

"'Tis this; that the soul, being forced to rejoice or be afflicted upon any occasion, is persuaded that what causes its pleasure or grief is a real and true thing, though at the same time it is not; and such is the nature of all sensible and visible things that are capable to occasion joy or grief."

"That is certain, Socrates."

"Are not these passions, then, the chief instruments particularly that imprison and mew up the soul within the body?"

"How's that, Socrates?"

"Every pleasure, every melancholy thought, being armed with a strong and keen nail, nails the soul to the body with such force that it becomes material and corporeal, and fancies there are no real and true objects but such as the body accounts so: for as it entertains the same opinions and pursues the same pleasures with the body, so it is obliged to the same actions and habits. For which reason it cannot descend in purity to the lower world, but is daubed all over with the pollution of the body itself, and quickly re-enters another body, where it takes root as if it had been sown, and puts a period to all commerce with the pure, simple, and divine essence."

"That is very certain, Socrates."

"These are the motives that oblige the true philosophers to make it their business to acquire temperance and fortitude, and not such motives as the vulgar think of. Are not you of my opinion, Cebes?"

"Yes, surely."

"All true philosophers will still be of that mind. Their souls will never entertain such a thought as if philosophy should disengage it to the end that when 'tis freed it should follow its pleasures, and give way to its fears and sorrows; that it should put on its chains again, and always want to begin again, like Penelope's web. On the contrary, it continues in a perfect tranquillity and freedom from passion, and always follows reason for its guide, without departing from its measures; it incessantly contemplates what is true, divine, immutable, and above opinion, being nourished by this pure truth: it is convinced that it ought to follow the same course of life while it is united to the body; and hopes that after death, being surrendered to that immortal being as its source, 'twill be freed from all the afflictions of the human nature. After such a life, and upon such principles, my dear Simmias and Cebes, what should the soul be afraid of? Shall it fear that upon its departure from the body the winds will dissipate it and run away with it, and that annihilation will be its fate?"

Socrates having thus spoken, he stopped for a while, seeming to be altogether intent upon what he had said. Most of us were in the same condition; Cebes and Simmias had a short conference together. At last Socrates, perceiving their conference, asked them what they were speaking of. "Do you think," says he, "that my arguments were lame? I think, indeed, there is room left for a great many doubts and objections, if any will take the pains to retail them out. If you are speaking of anything else I have nothing to say. But though you have no doubts, pray tell me freely whether you think of any better demonstration, and make me a companion in your inquiry, if you think I can assist you to compass your end."

"I'll tell you," says Simmias, "the naked truth. It is some time since Cebes and I thought of some doubts; and, being desirous to have them resolved, pushed on one another to propose them to you. But we were both afraid to importune you and propose disagreeable questions in the unseasonable hour of your present misfortune."

"Oh, my dear Simmias," replies Socrates, smiling, "certainly I should find great difficulty in persuading other men that I find no misfortune in my present circumstances, since I cannot get you to believe it. You think that upon the score of foreknowledge and divining I am infinitely inferior to the swans. When they perceive approaching death they sing more merrily than before, because of the joy they have in going to the God they serve. But men, through the fear of death, reproach the swans, in saying that they lament their death and tune their grief in sorrowful notes. They forget to make this reflection, that no fowl sings when 'tis hungry, or cold, or sad; nay, not the nightingale, the swallow, or the lapwing, whose music they say is a true lamentation and the effect of grief. But, after all, these fowls do not all sing out of grief; and far less the swans, which by reason of their belonging to Apollo are diviners, and sing more joyfully on the day of their death than before, as foreseeing the good that awaits them in the other world. And, as for me, I think I serve Apollo as well as they. I am consecrated to that God as well as they; I have received from our common Master the art of divining as well as they, and I am as little concerned for making my exit as they are. So that you may freely propose what doubts you please, and put questions to me as long as the eleven magistrates suffer me to be here."

"You say well, Socrates," replies Simmias; "since 'tis so I will suppose my doubts first, and then Cebes shall give in his. I agree with you that 'tis impossible, or, at least, very difficult, to know the truth in this life; and that it is the property of a lazy and dull head not to weigh exactly what he says or to supersede the examination before he has made all his efforts, and be obliged to give over by unsurmountable difficulties. For one of these two things must be done, we must either learn the truth from others or find it out ourselves. If both ways fail us, amidst all human reasons, we must pitch upon the strongest and most forcible, and trust to that as to a ship while we pass through this stormy sea, and endeavour to avoid its tempests and shelves; till we find out one more firm and sure, such as a promise or revelation upon which we may happily accomplish the voyage of this life as in a vessel that fears no danger. I shall therefore not be ashamed to put the questions to you, now that you allow me; and shall avoid the reproach I might one day cast upon myself of not having told you my thoughts upon this occasion. When I survey what you spoke to me and to Cebes I must own I do not think your proofs sufficient."

"Perhaps you have reason, my dear Simmias; but where does their insufficiency appear?"

"In this; that the same things might be asserted of the harmony of a harp. For one may reasonably say that the harmony of a harp, well stringed and well tuned, is invisible, immaterial, excellent, and divine; and that the instrument and its strings are the body, the compounded earthy and mortal matter. And if the instrument were cut in pieces or its strings broken, might not one with equal reason affirm that this harmony remains after the breaking of the harp and has no end ? For, since it is evident that the harp remains after the strings are broken, or that the strings, which are likewise mortal, continue after the harp is broken or dismounted, it must needs be impossible, might one say, that this immortal and divine harmony should perish before that which is mortal and earthly; nay, it is necessary that this harmony should continue to be without the least damage when the body of the harp and its strings are gone to nothing. For, without doubt, Socrates, you are sensible that we hold the soul to be something that resembles a harmony; and that as our body is a being composed of hot and cold, dry and moist, so our soul is nothing else but the harmony resulting from the just proportion of these mixed qualities. Now, if our soul is only a sort of harmony, 'tis evident that when our body is overstretched, or unbended by diseases, or any other disorder, of necessity our soul, with all its divinity, must come to an end, as well as the other harmonies which consist in sounds or are the effect of instruments; and that the remains of every body continue for a considerable time, till they be burnt or mouldered away. This, you see, Socrates, might be alleged in opposition to your arguments, that if the soul be only a mixture of the qualities of our body it perishes first in what we call death."

Then Socrates looked upon us all, one after another, as he did often, and began to smile. "Simmias speaks with reason," says he, "his question is well put; and if any one of you has a greater dexterity in answering his objections than I have, why do you not do it? For he seems thoroughly to understand both my arguments, and the exceptions they are liable to. But before we answer him, 'tis proper to hear what Cebes has to object, that while he speaks we may have time to think upon what we are to say; and after we have heard them both, that we may yield if their reasons are uniform and valid, and if otherwise, may stand by our principles to the utmost. Tell us, then, Cebes, what is it that hinders you from agreeing with what I have laid down?"

"I'll tell you," says Cebes; "your demonstration

seems to be lame and imperfect; it is faulty upon the same head that we took notice of before. That the soul has a being before its entrance into the body, is admirably well said, and I think sufficiently made out; but I can never be persuaded that it has likewise an existence after death. At the same time, I cannot subscribe to Simmias's allegation, that the soul is neither stronger nor more durable than the body, for to me it appears to be infinitely more excellent. But why, then, says the objection, do you refuse to believe it? Since you see with your eyes, that when a man is dead his weakest part remains still, is it not therefore absolutely necessary that the more durable part should last yet longer? Pray take notice if I answer this objection right. For to let you into my meaning, I must use resemblance or comparison, as well as Simmias. Your allegation, to my mind, is just the same, as if upon the death of an old tailor one should say, this tailor is not dead, he has a being still somewhere or other; and for proof of that, there's the suit of clothes he wore, which he made for himself, so that he's still in being. If any one should not be convinced by this proof, he would not fail to ask him, whether the man or the clothes he wears is most durable? To which, of necessity, he must answer that the man is; and upon this ground, your philosopher would pretend to demonstrate that since the less durable possession of the tailor is still in being, by stronger consequence he himself is so too. Now, my dear Simmias, the parallel is not just. Pray hear what I have to answer to it."

" 'Tis evident, at first view, that the objection is ridiculous. For the tailor, having used several suits of clothes, died after them, and only before the last suit, which he had not time to wear, and though the suit survived the man, if I may so speak, yet we cannot say the man is weaker or less durable than the suit of clothes. This simile is near enough, for as the man is to this suit of clothes, so is the soul to the body; and whoever applies to the soul and body what is said of the man and his suit of clothes will speak to the purpose. For he'll make the soul more durable, and the body a weaker being, and less capable to hold out for a long time. He'll add, that every soul wears several bodies, especially if it lives several years. For the body wastes while the man is yet alive, and the soul still forms to itself a new habit of body out of the former that decays: but when the last comes to die, it has then its last habit on, and dies before its consummation; and when the soul is dead, the body quickly betrays the weakness of its nature, since it corrupts and moulders away very speedily. So that we cannot put such confidence in your demonstration, as to hold it for a standing truth that our souls continue in being after death. For supposing it were granted that our soul has not a being antecedent to our birth, but that, for anything we know, the souls of some continue in being after death; and that 'tis very possible they may return again to the world, and be born again, so to speak, several times, and die at last; for the strength and advantage of the soul beyond the body, consists in this, that it can undergo several births, and wear several bodies one after another, as a man does a suit of clothes; supposing, I say, that all this were granted, still it cannot be denied, but that in all those repeated births it decays and wastes, and at last comes to an end in one of the deaths. However, 'tis impossible for any man to discern in which of the deaths 'tis totally sunk. Since things stand thus, whoever does not fear death must be senseless, unless he can demonstrate that the soul is altogether immortal and incorruptible. For otherwise every dying man must of necessity be afraid for his soul, for fear the body it is quitting be its last body, and it perishes without any hopes of return."

Having heard them propose these objections, we were very much troubled, as we afterwards told them, that at a time when we were just convinced by Socrates's arguments, they should come to amuse us with their objections, and throw us into a fit of unbelief and jealousy, not only of all that had been said to us by Socrates, but likewise of what he might say for the future; for we would always be apt to believe that either we were not proper judges of the points in debate, or else that his propositions were in themselves incredible.

Echec. Indeed, Phædo, I can easily pardon your trouble upon that account. For I myself, while I heard you relate the matter, was saying to myself, what shall we believe hereafter, since Socrates's arguments, which seemed so valid and convincing, are become doubtful and uncertain? In effect that objection of Simmias's, that the soul is only a harmony, moves me wonderfully, and always did so. It awakes in me the memory of my being formerly of the same opinion. So that my belief is unhinged, and I want new proofs to convince me that the soul does not die with the body. Wherefore, prithee tell me, Phædo, in the name of God, how Socrates came off, whether he seemed to be as much nettled as you, or if he maintained his opinion with his wonted temper; and in fine, whether his demonstration gave you full satisfaction, or seemed chargeable with imperfections? Pray tell me the whole story, without omitting the minutest circumstance.

Phædo. I protest to you, Echecrates, I admire Socrates all my lifetime, and upon this occasion admired him more than ever. That such a man as he had his answers in readiness is no great surprisal; but my greatest admiration was to see, in the first place, with what calmness, patience, and good humour he received the objections of these youngsters; and then how dexterously he perceived the impression they had made upon us, and cured us of the same He rallied us like men put to flight after a defeat, and inspired us with a fresh ardour to turn our heads and renew the charge.

Echec. How was that?

Phædo. I am about to tell you. As I sat at his right hand upon a little stool lower than his, he drew his hand over my head, and taking hold of my hair that hung down upon my shoulders, as he was wont to do for his diversion, "Phædo," says he, "will not you cut this pretty hair to-morrow?" "'Tis probable I shall," said I. "If you take my advice," said he, "you will not stay so long." "How do you mean?" said I. "Both you and I," continues he, "ought to cut our hair, if our opinion be so far dead that we cannot raise it again. Were I in your place, and defeated, I would make a vow, as the men of Argos did, never to wear my hair before I conquered these arguments of Simmias and Cebes." "But," said I, "Socrates, you have forgotten the old proverb, that Hercules himself is not able to engage two." "And why," says he, "do you not call on me to assist you as your Iolas, while 'tis yet time?" "And accordingly I do call on you," said I, "not as Hercules did Iolas, but as Iolas did Hercules." "'Tis no matter for that," says he, "'tis all one. Above all, let us be cautious to avoid one great fault." "What fault?" said I. "That," said he, "of being reason-haters, for such there are, as well as men-haters. The former is the greatest evil in the world, and arises from the same source with the hatred of man. For the latter comes from one man's plighting his faith for another man, without any precaution or inquiry, whom he always took for a true-hearted, solid, and trusty man, but finds him at last to be a false, faithless cheat; and thus being cheated in several such instances, by those whom he looked on as his best friends, and at last weary of being so often noosed, he equally hates all men, and is convinced there is not one that is not wicked and perfidious. Are not you sensible that this man-hating is formed at this rate by degrees?" "Yes, surely," said I. "Is it not a great scandal, then," continued he, "and a superlative crime, to converse with men without being acquainted with the art of trying them and knowing them? For if one were acquainted with this art, he would see how things stand, and would find that the good and the wicked are very rare, but those in the middle region swarm in infinite numbers."

"How do you say, Socrates?"

"I say, Phædo, the case of the good and bad is much the same with that of very large or very little men. Do not you see that there's nothing more uncommon than a very big or a very little man? The case is the same with reference to dogs, horses, and all other things; and may likewise be applied to swiftness and slowness, handsomeness and deformity, whiteness and blackness. Are not you convinced that in all these matters the two extremes are very uncommon, and the medium is very common?"

"I perceive it very plainly, Socrates."

"If a match were proposed for wickedness, would not there be very few that could pretend to the first rank?"

"That's very likely, Socrates."

"It is certainly so," replies he. "But upon this score the case of reason and men is not exactly the same. I'll follow you step by step. The only resemblance of the two lies in this, that when a man unskilled in the art of examination entertains a reason as true, and afterwards finds it to be false, whether it be so in itself or not, and when the same thing happens to him often—as indeed it does to those who amuse themselves in disputing with the sophisters, that contradict everything—he at last believes himself to be extraordinary well skilled, and fancies he's the only man that has perceived there's nothing true or certain, either in things or reasons, but that all is like Euripus, in a continual flux and reflux, and that nothing continues so much as one minute in the same state."

"That is the pure truth, Socrates."

"Is it not, then, a very deplorable misfortune, my dear Phædo, that while there are true, certain, and very comprehensive reasons, there should be men found who, after they have suffered them to pass, call them again in question upon hearing these frivolous disputes, where sometimes truth and falsehood comes uppermost; and instead of charging themselves without these doubts, or blaming their want of art, cast the blame at last upon the reasons themselves; and, being of a sour temper, pass their life in hating and calumniating all reason, and by that means rob themselves both of truth and knowledge?"

"That's certainly a most deplorable thing," said I.

"We ought to be very cautious," continues he, "that this misfortune be not our lot, and that we are not prepossessed by this thought, that there's nothing solid or true in all arguments whatsoever. We should rather be persuaded that 't is ourselves who are wanting in solidity and truth; and use our utmost efforts to recover that solidity and justness of thought. This is a duty incumbent upon you, who have time yet to live; and likewise upon me, who am about to die; and I am much afraid that upon this occasion I have been so far from acting the part of a true philosopher, that I have behaved myself like a disputant overborne with prejudice, as all those ignorants do who in their disputes do not mind the preception of the truth, but mean only to draw their hearers over to their opinions. The only difference between them and me is, that convincing my audience of the truth of what I advance is not my only aim—indeed, I shall be infinitely glad if that come to pass—but my chief scope is to persuade myself of the truth of these things; for I argue thus, my dear Phædo, and you'll find that this way of arguing is highly useful. If my propositions prove true, it is well done to believe them; and if after my death they be found false, I still reap that advantage in this life, that I have been less affected by evils which commonly accompany it. But I shall not remain long under this ignorance. If I were, I should reckon it a great misfortune; but by good luck it will quickly be dispelled. Being fortified by these thoughts, my dear Simmias and Cebes, I make account to answer your objections; and if you take my advice, you'll rely less upon the authority of Socrates than that of the truth. If what I am about to advance appear true, embrace it; if otherwise, attack it with all your force. Thus, I shall neither deceive myself, nor impose upon you by the influence of zeal and goodwill, or quit you like a wasp that leaves its sting in the wound it has made.

"To begin, then, pray see if I remember rightly what was objected. Simmias, as I take it, rejects our belief only because he fears our souls, notwithstanding their being divine and more excellent, will die before our bodies, as being only a sort of harmony. And, Cebes, if I mistake not, granted that the soul is more durable than the body, but thinks it possible that the soul, after having used several bodies, may die at last, when it quits the last body, and that this death of the soul is a true death. Are not these the two points I am to examine, my dear Simmias and Cebes?"

When they had all agreed that the objections were justly summed up, he continued thus :—" Do you absolutely reject all that I have said, or do you acknowledge part of it to be true?" They answered that they did not reject the whole. "But what," says he, "is your opinion of what I told you, viz., that learning is only remembrance, and that, by a necessary consequence, the soul must have an existence before its conjunction with the body?"

"As for me," replies Cebes, "I perceived the evidence of it at first view, and do not know any principles of more certainty and truth."

"I am of the same mind," says Simmias, "and should think it very strange if ever I changed my opinion."

"But, my dear Theban," continues Socrates, "you must needs change it, if you retain your opinion that harmony is compounded, and that the soul is a sort of harmony, arising from the due union of the qualities of the body; for 'tis presumed you would not believe yourself if you said that harmony has a being before those things of which it is composed."

"Sure enough," replies Simmias; "I would not believe myself if I did."

"Do not you see, then," continues Socrates, "that you are not of a piece with yourself when you say the soul had a being before it came to animate the body; and at the same time, that it is compounded of things that had not then an existence? Do not you compare the soul to a harmony? And is it not evident that the harp, the strings, and the very discordant sounds exist before the harmony, which is an effect that results from all these things that perishes sooner than they? Does this latter part of your discourse suit with the first?"

"Not at all," replies Simmias.

"And yet," continues Socrates, "if ever a discourse be all of a piece, it ought to be such when harmony is its subject."

"That's right," says Simmias.

"But yours is not so," continues Socrates. "Let's hear, then, which of these two opinions you side with: whether is learning only remembrance, or is the soul a sort of harmony?"

"I side with the first," replies Simmias.

"And that opinion I have explained to you,

without having any recourse to demonstrations full of similes and examples, which are rather colours of the truth, and therefore please the people best; but as for me, I am of opinion that all discourses proving their point by similes are full of vanity, and apt to seduce and deceive, unless one be very cautious, whether it relate to geometry or any other science; whereas the discourse I made for proving that knowledge is remembrance is grounded upon a very credible hypothesis; for I told you that the soul exists as well as its essence before it comes to animate the body. By essence, I mean the principle from which it derives its being, which has no other name but that which is. And this proof I take to be good and sufficient."

"By that reason," says Simmias, "I must not listen either to myself or others, who assert the soul to be a sort of harmony."

"In earnest, Simmias," replies Socrates, "do you think that a harmony, or any other composure, can be anything different from the parts of which it is compounded?"

"By no means, Socrates."

"Or, can it do or suffer what those parts do not?"

Simmias answered that it could not.

"Then," says Socrates, "a harmony does not precede, but follow the thing it is composed of; and it cannot have sounds and motions, or anything else contrary to its parts."

"No, surely," replies Simmias.

"But what," continues Socrates, "is not all harmony only such in proportion to the concord of its parts?"

"I do not well understand you," says Simmias.

"I mean, according as the parts have more or less of concord, the harmony is more or less a harmony, is it not?"

"Yes, surely."

"Can we say of the soul, at the same rate, that a small difference makes a soul to be more or less a soul?"

"No, surely, Socrates."

"How is it, then, in the name of God? Do not we say, for example, that such a soul endowed with understanding and virtue is good, and another filled with folly and mischief is wicked? Is not this right?"

"Yes, surely," quoth Simmias.

"But those who hold the soul to be a harmony, what will they call these qualities of the soul, that vice, and that virtue? Will they say, the one's harmony, and the other discord? That a virtuous and good soul, being harmony in its nature, is entitled to another harmony, and that a vicious wicked soul wants that addition, harmony?"

"I cannot be positive," replies Simmias; "but indeed 'tis very probable the patrons of that opinion may advance some such thing."

"But we concluded, that one soul is not more or less a soul than another; that is, that it is not more or less a harmony, than another harmony."

"I own it," says Simmias.

"And since it is not more or less a harmony then it has not more or less concord? Is it not so?"

"Yes, surely, Socrates."

"And since it has not more or less of concord, can one have more harmony than another, or must the harmony of them all be equal?"

"Questionless it must be equal."

"Since one soul cannot be more or less a soul than another, by the same reason, it cannot have more or less of concord."

"That's true."

"Then it follows necessarily that one soul cannot have either more harmony or discord than another?"

"I agree to it."

"And by consequence, since the soul is of that nature, it cannot have more virtue or vice than another; if so be that vice is discord, and virtue harmony?"

"That is a standing truth," says Simmias.

"Or, would not right reason rather say that vice could find no place in the soul, if so be the soul is harmony? for harmony, continuing in its perfect nature, is not capable of discord."

"There is no question of that."

"In like manner the soul, while perfectly a soul, is not capable of vice."

"According to the principles we agreed upon, I cannot see how it should."

"From the same very principles it will follow, that the souls of all animals are equally good, since they are equally souls."

'So I think," says Simmias.

"But do you think that it stands with right reason, if the hypothesis of the soul's being a harmony be true?"

"No, surely, Socrates."

"Then I ask you, Simmias, if of all the parts of a man the soul is not best entitled to command, especially when she is prudent and wise?"

"There is no other part can pretend to it."

"Does it command by giving way to the passions of the body, or by resisting them? As, for example, when the body is seized with thirst in the cold fit of a fever, does not the soul restrain it from drinking? Or when 'tis hungry, does it not restrain from eating? As well as in a thousand other instances, which manifestly show that the soul curbs the passions of the body. Is it not so?"

"Without question."

"But we agreed above that the soul being a sort of harmony, can never sound contrary to the sound of those things which arise, or lower, or move it, nor have other passions different from those of its parts; and that it is necessarily obliged to follow them, as being incapable to guide them."

" 'Tis certain we agreed upon that," says Simmias; "how could we avoid it?"

"But," says Socrates, "is it not evident that the conduct of the soul is the downright contrary? That it governs and rules those very things which are alleged for ingredients in its composition; that it thwarts and attacks them almost all its lifetime; that it is every way their mistress, punishing and repressing some by the harder measures of pain, school-exercises, and physic; and treating others more gently, as contenting itself with threatening or insulting over its lusts, passion, and fear. In a word, we see the soul speaks to the body, as something of a different nature from itself, which Homer was sensible of, when in his Odyssey, he tells that ' Ulysses beating his breast, rebuked his heart, and said to it, Support thyself, thou hast stood out against harder and more difficult things than these.' "

"Do you think the poet spoke that under the apprehensions of the soul's being a harmony to be managed and conducted by the body? Or do you not rather believe that he knew it was the soul's part to command, and that it is of a nature more divine than harmony?"

"Yes, Socrates; I swear I am persuaded Homer knew that truth."

"And, by consequence, my dear Simmias," continues Socrates, "there is not the least colour of reason for the soul's being a harmony; should we assert it to be such we should contradict both Homer, that divine poet, and likewise ourselves." Simmias yielded, and Socrates proceeded thus.

"I think we have sufficiently tempered and moderated this Theban harmony, so that it will do us no harm. But Cebes, how shall we do to appease and disarm this Cadmus? How shall we hit on a discourse duly qualified with a persuasive force?"

"If you'll be at the pains, Socrates, you can easily find such a discourse. The last you had against the harmony of the soul moved me mightily, and indeed beyond my expectation : for when Simmias proposed his doubts, I thought nothing short of a prodigy or miracle could solve them, and I was mightily surprised when I saw he could not stand the first attack. So that now it will be no surprisal to me to see Cadmus undergo the same fate."

"My dear Cebes," replies Socrates, "do not you speak too big upon the matter, lest envy should overturn all I have said, and render it useless and ineffectual. But that's in the hands of God. As for us, let us approach one another, as Homer says, and try our strength and arms. What you want comes all to this point: You would have the immortality and incorruptibility of the soul demonstrated, to the end that a philosopher who dies bravely in the hopes of being infinitely more happy in the other world than in this, may not hope in vain. You say, the soul's being a durable and divine substance, existing before its joining the body, does not conclude its immortality ; and the only inference that it will bear is, that it lasts a great while longer, and was in being many ages before us, during which it knew and did several things, but without immortality; for on the contrary, the first minute of its descent into the body is the commencement of its death, or, as it were, a disease to it: for it passes this life in anguish and trouble, and at last is quite swallowed up and annihilated by what we call death. You add that 'tis the same thing, whether it animates a body only once, or returns to it several times, since that does not alter the occasion of our fears, forasmuch as all wise men ought still to fear death, while they are uncertain of the immortality of their souls. This, I take it, is the sum of what you said; and I repeat it so often, on purpose that nothing may escape my view, and that you may have the opportunity of adding or impairing as you please."

"At present," says Cebes, "I have nothing to alter; that is the just sum of all I have yet said."

Socrates was silent a pretty while, as being drowned in profound meditation. At last, "Cebes," says he, "'tis truly not a small matter that you demand: for in order to a just satisfaction, there's a necessity of making a narrow inquiry into the cause of generation and corruption. If you please, I'll tell you what happened to me upon this very matter; and if what I say seem useful to you, you shall be at liberty to make use of it to support your sentiments."

"With all my heart," says Simmias.

"Pray give ear, then," says Socrates: "In my youth I had an insatiable desire to learn that science which is called natural history; for I thought it was something great and divine to know the causes of every thing, of their generation, death, and existence. And I spared no pains, nor omitted any means, for trying, in the first place, if a certain corruption of hot and cold will, as some pretend, give being and nourishment to animals; if the blood makes the thought, if air or fire, or the brain alone is the cause of our senses of seeing, hearing, smelling, &c., if memory and opinion take their rise from these senses, and if knowledge be the result of memory and opinion. Then I wanted to know the causes of their corruption, and extended my curiosity both to the heavens and the cavities of the earth, and would fain have known the cause of all the phenomena we meet with. At last, after a great deal of trouble, I found myself strangely unqualified for such inquiries; and of this I am about to give you a sensible proof. This fine study made me so blind in the things I knew more evidently before, according to my own and other persons' thoughts, that I quite forgot all that I had known from several subjects, particularly that of a man's growth. I thought 'twas evident to the whole world that a man grows only by eating and drinking; for flesh being added to flesh, bones to bones, and all the other parts joined to their similar parts by nourishment, make a small bulk to swell and grow, so that a little man becomes a large. This was my thought, do you think 'twas just?"

"Yes, surely," replies Cebes.

"Mind what follows," says Socrates. "I thought likewise that I knew the reason why one man is taller than another by the head, and one horse higher than another: and with reference to plainer and more sensible things, I thought, for instance, that ten was more than eight, because two was added to it; and that two cubits were larger than one because they contained one-half more."

"And what are your present thoughts of those things?"

"I am so far," replies Socrates, "from thinking that I know the cause of all these things, that when one is added to one, I do not believe I can tell whether it is that very one to which the other is added that becomes two, or whether the one is added, and the one to which the addition was made make two together? For, in their separate state, each of them was one, and not two, and after their being placed one by the other they became two. Neither can I tell how, upon the division of anything, what was formerly one becomes two, from the very minute of division; for that cause is quite contrary to that which makes one and one become two. There, this one and this one become two by reason of their being placed near, and added the one to the other; but here this one thing becomes two by reason of its division and separation. Far less do I pretend to know whence this one thing comes, and by this method, *i.e.*, by physical reasons, I cannot fin l how the least thing takes rise or perishes, or how it exists. But without so much ceremony, I mix another method of my own with this, for by this I can learn nothing. Having one day heard somebody reading a book of Anaxagoras's, who said the divine intellect was the cause of all beings, and drew them upon their proper ranks and classes, I was ravished with joy. I perceived there was nothing more certain than this principle, that the intellect is the cause of all things. For I justly thought that this intellect, having methodised all things and ranked them in their classes, planting everything in the place and condition that was best and most useful to it, in which it could best do and suffer whatever the intellect had allotted to it; and I apprehended that the result of this principle was, that the only thing a man ought to look for, either for himself or others, is this better and more useful thing; for having once found what is best and most useful, he'll necessarily know what is worst, since there is but one knowledge both for the one and the other.

"Upon this score I was infinitely glad that I had found such a master as Anaxagoras, who I hoped would give a satisfactory account of the cause of all things; and would not only tell me, for instance, that the earth is broad or round, but likewise assign the necessary cause, obliging it to be so: who would point out to me what is best, and at the same time give me to understand why it was so. In like manner, if he affirmed the seat of the earth to be in the centre of the world, I expected he would give me a reason why it was so; and after I should have received sufficient instruction from him, designed never to admit of any other cause for a principle.

"I prepared some question to be put to him concerning the sun, moon, and the stars, in order to know the reasons of their revolutions, motions, and other accidents, and why what each of them does is always the best: for I could not imagine that after he had told me that the intellect ranked them, and drew them up in order, he could give me no other reason of that order than this, that it was best. And I flattered myself with hopes, that after he had assigned both the general and particular causes, he would give me to know wherein the particular good of every individual thing, as well as the common good of all things, consists. I would not have parted with these hopes for all the treasures of the world.

"So I bought his books with a great deal of impatience, and made it my business to peruse them as soon as possible I could, in order to a speedy knowledge of the good and evil of all this; but I found myself frustrated of my mighty hopes, for as soon as I had made a small progress in the perusal I found the author made no use of this intellect, and assigned no reason of that fine order and disposition; but assigned, as causes, the air, whirlwinds, the waters, and other things equally absurd.

"His whole performance seemed to reach no farther, than if a man should say, that Socrates does all by the intellect; and after that, meaning to give a reason for my actions, should say, for instance, to-day I am set upon my bed, because my body is composed of bones and nerves; the bones being hard and solid are separated by the joints; and the nerves, being capable to bend and unbend themselves, tie the bones to the flesh and the skin, which receives and includes both the one and the other; that the bones being disengaged at the joints, the nerves, which bend and unbend, enable me to fold my legs as you see; and that, forsooth, is the reason that I sit in this posture. Or if a man pretending to assign the cause of my present conference with you should insist only upon the second causes, the voice, the air, hearing, and such other things, and should take no notice of the true cause, viz., that the Athenians thought it fit to condemn me, and that by the same reason I thought it fitter for me to be here, and patiently wait the execution of my sentence, for I can safely swear that these nerves and these bones should long ere now have been translated to Megara, or Bœotia, if that had been fitted for me, and if I had not been persuaded that it was better and fitter for me to endure the punishment I am doomed to by my country, than to flee like a slave or a banished person. As I take it, 'tis highly ridiculous to assign such causes upon such an occasion, and to rest satisfied in them.

"If it be replied, that without bones and nerves, and such other things, I could not do what I mean to do, the allegation is true. But it savours of the greatest absurdity to fancy that these bones or nerves should be the cause of my actions, rather than the choice of what is best; and that my intellect is employed on that score, for that were to sink the difference between the cause and the thing, without which the cause could not be such. And yet the vulgar people, who take things by hearsay, and see by other people's eyes, as if they walked in thick darkness, take the true cause of things to be of that nature. Pursuant to this notion, some surround the earth with a vortex that turns eternally round, and suppose it to be fixed in the centre of the universe; others conceive it to be a broad and large trough, which has the air for its base and foundation. And as for the power of Him who ranked and disposed of everything to its best advantage, that is not in their view, and they don't believe that He is entitled to any divine virtue. They fancy they know of a stronger and more immortal Atlas, more capable to support all things. And this good and immortal tie that is only capable to unite and comprehend all things, they take for a chimera.

"I am of their mind, but would willingly 'list myself a disciple to any that could tell me the cause, let it be what it will. But since I could not compass the knowledge of it, neither by myself nor others, if you please I'll give you an account of a second trial I made in order to find it."

"I am very desirous to hear it," says Cebes.

"After I had wearied myself in examining all things, I thought it my duty to be cautious of avoiding what happens to those who contemplate an eclipse of the sun; for they lose the sight of it, unless they be careful to view its reflection in water or any other medium. A thought much like to that came into my head, and I feared I should lose the eyes of my soul if I viewed objects with the eyes of my body, or employed any of my senses in endeavouring to know them. I thought I should have recourse to reason, and contemplate the truth of all things as reflected from it. 'Tis possible the simile I use in explaining myself is not very just, for I myself cannot affirm that he who beholds things in the glass of reason sees them more by reflection and similitude than he who beholds them in their operations. However, the way I followed was this: from that time forward I grounded all upon the reason that seemed to be best, and took all for truth that I found conformable to it, whether in things or causes. And what was not conformable I rejected, as being false. I'll explain my meaning more distinctly, for I fancy you do not yet understand me."

"I'll swear," says Cebes, "I do not well understand you."

"But after all," says Socrates, "I advance no new thing. This is no more than what I have said a thousand times, and particularly in the foregoing dispute; for all that I aim at is to demonstrate what sort of cause this is that I sought after so carefully. I begin with his qualities, which are so much talked of, and which I take for the foundation. I say, then, there is something that is good, fine, just, and great of itself. If you grant me this principle, I hope by it to demonstrate the cause, and make out the immortality of the soul."

"I grant it," says Cebes; "you cannot be too quick in perfecting your demonstration."

"Mind what follows, and see if you agree to it as I take it. If there is anything fine, besides fineness itself, it must be such by partaking of that first good; and so of all the other qualities. Are you of this opinion?"

"I am."

"I protest," continues Socrates, "I cannot well understand all the other learned causes that are commonly given us. But if any man ask me what makes a thing fine, whether the liveliness of its colours, or the just proportion of its parts, and the like, I waive all these plausible reasons, which serve only to confound me, and without ceremony or art, make answer, and perhaps too simply, that its fineness is only owing to the presence, or approach, or communication of the original fine being, whatever be the way of that communcation. For I am not yet certain in what manner it is; I only know certainly that all these fine things are rendered such by the presence of this fine being. While I stand by this principle I reckon I cannot be deceived, and I am persuaded that I may safely make answer to all questions whatsoever, that all fine things owe their fineness to the presence of the above-mentioned being. Are not you of the same mind?"

"Yes, surely, Socrates."

"Are not great and small things rendered such in like manner? If one told you that such a thing is larger than another by the head, would not you think the expression far from being exact? and would not you make answer, that whatever is larger is rendered such by magnitude itself, and what is smaller owes its littleness to littleness itself? For if you said that such a thing is greater or smaller than another by the head, I fancy you would fear being censured for making both the greater and lesser thing to be such by the same cause; and besides, for using such an expression as seems to imply that the head, which is a small part, makes the largeness of the greater, which in effect is a monster; for what can be more absurd than to say that a small matter makes a thing large? Would not you fear such objections?"

"Yes, surely," replies Cebes, smiling.

"By the same reason would not you be afraid to say that ten are more than eight, and surpasses it by two? and would not you rather say that ten are more than eight by quantity? In like manner, of two cubits, would not you say they are larger than one by magnitude, rather than by the half? For still there's the same occasion of fear."

"You say well."

"But when one is added to one, or a thing divided into halves, would not you avoid saying that in the former case addition makes one and one two? and in the latter, division makes one thing become two? And would not you protest that you know no other cause of the existence of things than the participation of the essence that's peculiar to every subject, and consequently no other reason why one and one makes two, but the participation of quality, as one is one by the participation of unity? Would not you discard these additions, divisions, and all the other fine answers, and leave them to those who know more than you do? And, for fear of your own shadow, as the proverb goes, or rather of your ignorance, would not you confine yourself to this principle? And if any one attacked it, would not you let it stand without deigning him an answer till you had surveyed all the consequences to see if they are of a piece or not? And if afterwards you should be obliged to give a reason for them, would not you do it by having recourse to some of these other hypotheses that should appear to be the best, and so proceed from hypothesis to hypothesis till you lighted upon somebody that satisfied you as being a sure and standing truth? At the same time, you would be loth to perplex and confound all things, as those disputants do who call all things in question? 'Tis true, these disputants perhaps are not much concerned for the truth, and by thus mingling and perplexing all things by an effect of their profound knowledge they are sure to please themselves. But as for you, if you are true philosophers, you will do as I say."

Simmias and Cebes jointly replied, "That he said well."

Echec. Indeed, Phædo, I think it no wonder; for to my mind Socrates explained his principles with a wonderful neatness sufficient to make an impression upon any man of common sense.

Phædo. All the audience thought the same.

Echec. Even we who have it only at second hand find it so. But what was said next?

Phædo. If I remember right, after they had granted that the species of things have a real subsistence, and that the things participating of their nature take their denomination from them, then, I say, Socrates interrogated Cebes as follows:—

"If your principle be true, when you say Simmias is larger than Socrates and lesser than Phædo, do not you imply that both magnitude and littleness are lodged at the same time in Simmias?"

"Yes," replies Cebes.

"But do not you own that this proposition, Simmias is bigger than Socrates, is not absolutely and in itself true? For Simmias is not bigger because he is Simmias, but because he is possessed of magnitude. Neither is Simmias lesser than Phædo because Phædo is Phædo, but because Phædo is big when compared to Simmias, who is little."

"That's true."

"Thus," continues Socrates, "Simmias is called both big and little, as being between two; by partaking of bigness he is bigger than Socrates, and by partaking also of littleness he is lesser than Phædo." Then he smiled, and said, "Methinks I have insisted too long on these things, but I should not have amused myself with these large strokes had it not been to convince you more effectually of the truth of my principle. For, as I take it, not only magnitude itself cannot be at the same time big and small, but, besides, the magnitude that is in us does not admit of littleness, and has no mind to be surpassed, for either the magnitude flees and yields its place when it sees its enemy approaching, or else it vanishes and perishes entirely; and, when once it has received it, it desires to continue as it is. As I, for instance, having received littleness, while I am as you see me, cannot but be little. For that which is big does never attempt to be little. And in like manner littleness never encroaches upon magnitude. In a word, any of the contraries, while it is what it is, is never to be found with its contrary; but either disappears or perishes when the other comes in."

Cebes agreed to it, but one of the company, I forgot who, addressed himself to Socrates thus: " In the name of all the gods, did not you say contrary to what you now advance? Did not you conclude upon this, that greater things take rise from the lesser, and the lesser from the greater; and, in a word, that contraries do still produce their contraries? Whereas now, as I take it, you allege that can never be."

Whereupon Socrates put his head further out of the bed, and having heard the objection, said to him, "Indeed, you do well to put us in mind of what we said; but you do not perceive the difference between the former and the latter. In the former we asserted that every contrary owes its being to its contrary, and in the latter we teach that a contrary is never contrary to itself, neither in us, nor in the course of nature. There we spoke of things that had contraries, meaning to call every one of them by their proper names, but here we speak of such things as give a denomination to their subjects, which, we told you, could never admit of their contraries." Then turning to Cebes, "Did not this objection," says he, "likewise give you some trouble?"

"No, indeed, Socrates," replies Cebes; "I can assure you that few things are capable to trouble me at present."

"Then we agreed upon this simple proposition," says Socrates, "that a contrary can never be contrary to itself."

"That is true," says Cebes.

"But what do you say to this? Is cold and heat anything?"

"Yes, surely."

"What, is it like snow and fire?"

"No, surely, Socrates."

"Then you own that heat is different from fire, and cold from snow?"

"Without question, Socrates."

"I believe you'll likewise own that when the snow receives heat it is no more what it was, but either gives way, or disappears for good and all, when the heat approaches. In like manner the fire will either yield or be extinguished when the cold prevails upon it; for then it cannot be fire and cold together."

"'Tis so," says Cebes.

"There are also some contraries that not only give name to their species, but likewise impart it to other things different from it, which preserve its figure and form while they have a being. For instance, must not an odd thing have always the same name?"

"Yes, surely."

"Is that the only thing that is so called? Or, is not there some other things different from it, which must needs be called by the same name, by reason that it belongs to its nature never to be without odds? For instance, must not the ternary number be called not only by its own name, but likewise by the name of an odd number; though at the same time to be odd and to be three are two different things? Now, such is the nature of the number three, five, and all other odd numbers; each of them is always odd, and yet their nature is not the same with the nature of the odd. In like manner, even numbers, such as two, four, eight, are all of them even, though at the same time their nature is not that of the even. Do not you own this?"

"How can I do otherwise?" says Cebes.

"Pray, mind what I infer from hence. 'Tis, that not only these contraries, which are incapable of receiving their contraries, but all other things which are not opposite one to another, and yet have always their contraries; all these things, I say, are incapable of receiving a form opposite to their own; and either disappear to perish upon the appearance of the opposite form. For instance: Number three will sink a thousand times rather than become an even number, while it continues to be three. Is it not so?"

"Yes, surely," replies Cebes.

"But after all," says Socrates, "two are not contrary to three."

"No, surely."

"Then the contrary species are not the only things that refuse admission to their contraries; since, as you see other things that are not contrary cannot abide the approach of that which has the least shadow of contrariety."

"That is certain."

"Do you desire, then, that I should define them as clear as possible?"

"Ay, with all my heart, Socrates."

"Must not contraries be such things as give such a form to that in which they are lodged, that it is not capable of giving admission to another that's contrary to them?"

"How do you say?"

"I say as I said but now: Wherever the idea or form of three is lodged, that thing must of necessity continue, not only to be three, but to be odd."

"Who doubts that?"

" And by consequence 'tis impossible for the idea or form that's contrary to its constituent form, ever to approach."

" That's a plain case."

" Well, is not the constituent form an odd ? "

" Yes."

" Is not even the form that's contrary to odd ? "

" Yes."

" Then the form of even is never lodged in three ? "

" No, surely."

" Then three is incapable of being even."

" Most certainly."

" And that, because three is odd ? "

" Yes, surely."

" Now, this is the conclusion I meant to prove, that some things that are not contrary to one another are as incapable of that other thing, as if it were truly a contrary; as, for instance, though three is not contrary to an even number, yet it can never admit of it. For two brings always something contrary to an odd number, like fire to cold, and several other things. Would not you agree, then, to this definition, that a contrary does not only refuse admission to its contrary, but likewise to that which, being not contrary, brings upon it something of a contrary name, which by that sort of contrariety destroys its form?"

"I pray you let me hear that again," says Cebes; "for 'tis worth the while to hear it often."

"I say number five will never be an even number; just as ten, which is its double, will never be odd; no more than three-fourths, or a third part, or any other part of a whole, will ever admit of the form and idea of the whole. Do you understand me? do you take me up, and do you agree with what I say?"

"I understand you; I apprehend you to a miracle; and I agree with you too."

"Since you understand me," says Socrates, " pray answer me as I do you; that is, answer me, not what I ask, but something else, according to the idea and example I have given you; I mean, that besides the true and certain way of answering spoken of already, I have yet another in my view that springs from that, and is fully as sure. For instance, if you ask me what it is that being in the body, makes it hot, I would not give you this ignorant, though sure answer, that 'tis heat; but would draw a more particular answer from what we have been speaking of, and would tell you that it is fire. And if you should ask what it is that makes the body sick, I would not say 'twas the disease, but the fever. If you ask me what makes a number odd, I would not tell you that it is the oddness, but unity; and so of the rest. Do you understand what I mean?"

"I understand you perfectly well," replies Cebes.

"Answer me, then," continues Socrates; "what makes the body live?"

"The soul."

"Is the soul always the same?"

"How would it be otherwise?"

"Does the soul, then, carry life along with it into all the bodies it enters?"

"Most certainly."

"Is there anything that's contrary to life, or is there nothing?"

"Yes, death is the contrary of life."

"Then the soul will never receive that which is contrary to what it carries in its bosom; that's a necessary consequence from our principles."

"'Tis a plain consequence," says Cebes.

"But what name do we give to that which refuses admission to the idea and form of evenness?"

"'Tis the odd number."

"How do we call that which never receives justice, and that which never receives good?"

"The one is called injustice, and the other evil."

"And how do you call that which never admits of death?"

"Immortal."

"Does the soul admit of death?"

"No."

"Then the soul is immortal."

"Most certainly."

"Is that fully demonstrated, or was the demonstration imperfect?"

"It is fully made out, Socrates."

"If an odd number of necessity were incorruptible, would not three be so too?"

"Who doubts it?"

"If whatever is without heat were necessarily incorruptible, would not snow, when put to the fire, withdraw itself safe from the danger? For since it cannot perish, it will never receive the heat, notwithstanding its being held to the fire."

"What you say is true."

"In like manner, if that which is not susceptible of cold were by a natural necessity exempted from perishing, though a whole river were thrown upon the fire, it would never go out, but on the contrary would come off with its full force."

"There is an absolute necessity for that," says Cebes.

"Then of necessity we must say the same of what is immortal. If that which is immortal is incorruptible, though death approach to the soul, it shall never fall in the attack; for, as we said but now, the soul will never receive death, and will never die, just as three, or any odd number, will never be even; fire will never be cold, nor its heat be turned to coldness.

"Perhaps some may answer that 'tis true the odd can never become even, by the accession of what is even, while it continues odd; but what should hinder the even to take up the room of the odd when it comes to perish? To this objection it cannot be answered that the odd does not perish, for it is incorruptible. Had we established its incorruptibility, we should justly have maintained, that notwithstanding the attacks of the even, the odd of three would still come off without loss; and we should have asserted the same of fire, heat, and such other things, should not we?"

"Most certainly," says Cebes.

"And, by consequence, if we agree upon this, that every immortal thing is incorruptible, it will necessarily follow, not only that the soul is immortal, but that it is incorruptible. And if we cannot agree upon that, we must look out for another proof."

"There is no occasion for that, Socrates," replies Cebes; "for what is it that should avoid corruption and death, if an immortal and eternal being be liable to them?"

"All the world will agree," says Socrates, "that God, and life itself, and whatever 'tis that is immortal, does not perish."

"At least," says Cebes, "all men will profess so."

"The consequence is absolutely necessary and certain. And by consequence," continues Socrates, "when a man comes to die, his mortal and corruptible part dies; but the immortal part goes off safe, and triumphs over death."

"That's plain and evident."

"Then, my dear Cebes, if there be any such thing as an immortal and incorruptible being, such is the soul; and by consequence our souls shall live hereafter."

"I have nothing to object," says Cebes, "and cannot but yield to your arguments. But if Simmias, or any of the company, has anything to offer, they'll do well not to stifle it; for when will they find another occasion for discoursing and satisfying themselves upon these important subjects?"

"For my part," says Simmias, "I cannot but subscribe to what Socrates has said. But I own that the greatness of the subject, and the natural weakness of man, occasion within me a sort of distrust and incredulity."

"You have not only spoken well," says Socrates, "but besides, notwithstanding the apparent certainty of our first hypothesis, 'tis needful you should resume them, in order to a more leisurely view, and to convince yourself more clearly and effectually. If you understand them sufficiently, you'll willingly second my thoughts as much as possible for a man to do: and when you are once fully convinced, you'll need no other proof."

"That's well said," replies Cebes.

"There's one thing more, my friends, that is a very just thought, viz., that if the soul is immortal, it stands in need of cultivating and improvement, not only in the time that we call the time of life, but for the future, or what we call the time of eternity; for if you think justly upon this point you'll find it very dangerous to neglect the soul. Were death the dissolution of the whole man, it would be a great advantage to the wicked after death to be rid at once of their body, their soul, and their vices. But forasmuch as the soul is immortal, the only way to avoid those evils and obtain salvation is to become good and wise: for it carries nothing along with it but its good or bad actions, and its virtues or vices, which are the cause of its eternal happiness or misery, commencing from the first minute of its arrival in the other world. And 'tis said that after the death of every individual person, the Demon or Genius, that was partner with it and conducted it during life, leads it to a certain place, where all the dead are obliged to appear, in order to be judged, and from thence are conducted by a guide to the world below. And, after they have there received their good or bad deserts, and continued there their appointed time, another conductor brings them back to this life, after several revolutions of ages. Now this road is not a plain united road, else there would be no occasion for guides, and nobody would miss their way; but there are several by-ways and cross-ways, as I conjecture from the method of our sacrifices and religious ceremonies. So that a temperate, wise soul follows its guide, and is not ignorant of what happens to it; but the soul that's nailed to its body, as I said just now, that is inflamed with the love of it, and has been long its slave, after much struggling and suffering in this visible world, is at last dragged along against its will by the Demon allotted for its guide. And when it arrives at that rendezvous of all souls, if it has been guilty of any impurity, or polluted with murder, or has committed any of those atrocious crimes that desperate and lost souls are commonly guilty of, the other souls abhor it, and avoid its company; it finds neither companion nor guide, but wanders in a fearful solitude and horrible desert, till after a certain time necessity drags it into the mansions it deserves; whereas the temperate and pure soul has the gods themselves for its guides and conductors, and goes to cohabit with them in the mansions of pleasure prepared for it. For, my friends, there are several marvellous places in the earth: and 'tis not at all such as the describers of it are wont to make it, as I was taught by one who knew it very well.",

"How do you say, Socrates?" says Simmias, interrupting him. "I have likewise heard several things of the earth, but not what you have heard. Wherefore I wish you would be pleased to tell us what you know."

"To recount that to you, my dear Simmias, I do not believe we have any occasion for Glaucus's art. But to make out the truth of it is a more difficult matter, and I question if all Glaucus's art can reach it. Such an attempt is not only above my reach, but supposing it were not, the short time I have left me will not suffer me to embark in so long a discourse. All that I can do is to give you a general idea of this earth, and the places it contains."

"That will be enough," says Simmias.

"In the first place," continues Socrates, "I am persuaded that if the earth is placed in the middle of heaven (the air), as they say it is, it stands in no need of air, or any other support to prevent its fall; for heaven itself is wrapped equally about it, and its own equilibrium is in the middle of a thing that presses equally upon it, cannot incline to either side, and consequently stands firm and immovable. This I am convinced of."

OF THE IMMORTALITY OF THE SOUL. 171

"You have reason to be so," replies Simmias.

"I am farther persuaded that the earth is very large and spacious, and that we only inhabit that part of it which reaches from the river Phasis to the Straits of Gibraltar, upon which we are scattered like so many ants dwelling in holes, or like frogs that reside in some marsh near the sea. There are several other nations that inhabit its other parts that are unknown to us; for all over the earth there are holes of all sizes and figures, always filled with gross air, and covered with thick clouds, and overflown by the waters that rush in on all sides.

"There is another pure earth above the pure heaven where the stars are, which is commonly called Æther. The earth we inhabit is properly nothing else but the sediment of the other, and its grosser part which flows continually into those holes. We are immured in those cells, though we are not sensible of it, and fancy we inhabit the upper part of the pure earth, much after the same rate as if one living in the depths of the sea should fancy his habitation to be above the waters, and when he sees the sun and other stars through the waters, should fancy the sea to be the heavens, and by reason of his heaviness and weakness, having never put forth his sea head or raised himself above the waters, should never know that the place we inhabit is purer and nearer than his, and should never meet with any person to inform him. This is just our condition; we are mewed up within some hole of the earth, and fancy we live at the top of all: we take the air for the true heavens, in which the stars run their rounds. And the cause of our mistake is our heaviness and weakness, that keep us from surmounting this thick and muddy air. If any could mount up with wings to the upper surface, he would no sooner put his head out of the gross air but he would behold what's transacted in those blessed mansions, just as the fishes skipping above the surface of the waters see what's done in the air in which we breathe. And if he were a man fit for long contemplation, he would find it to be the true heaven and the true light: in a word, to be the true earth. For this earth that we inhabit, those stones, and all places are entirely corrupted and gnawed, just as whatever is in the sea is corroded by the sharpness of the salts. And the sea produces nothing that's perfect or valuable. It contains nothing but caves and mud : and wherever any ground is found, there's nothing but deep sloughs, nothing comparable to what we have here. Now the things in the other mansions are more above what we have here, than what we have here is above what we meet with in the sea. And in order to make you conceive the beauty of this pure earth situated in the heavens, if you please, I'll tell you a pretty story that's worth your hearing."

" We shall hear it," says Simmias, "with a great deal of pleasure."

"First of all, my dear Simmias," continued Socrates, " if one looks upon this earth from a high place, they say it looks like one of our packs covered with twelve welts of different colours. For it is varied with a greater number of different colours, of which those made use of by our painters are but sorry patterns. For the colours of this earth are infinitely more clean and lively. One is an admirable purple; another a colour of gold, more sparkling than gold itself; a third a white more lively than the snow; and so on of all the rest, the beauty whereof leaves our colours here far behind it. The chinks of this earth are filled with water and air, which make up an infinity of admirable shadows, so wonderfully diversified by that infinite variety of colours.

"In this so perfect an earth everything has a perfection answerable to its qualities. The trees, flowers, fruits, and mountains are charmingly beautiful; they produce all sorts of precious stones of an incomparable perfection, clearness, and splendour; those we esteem so much here, such as emeralds, jasper, and sapphire, are but small parcels of them. There is not one in that blessed earth that is not infinitely more pretty than of ours. The cause of all which is, that all these precious stones are pure, neither gnawed nor spoiled by the sharpness of the salts, or the corruption of the sediment or dregs that fall from thence into our lower earth, where they assemble, and infect not only the stones and the earth, but the plants and animals, with all sorts of pollution and diseases.

"Besides all these beauties now mentioned, this blessed earth is enriched with gold and silver, which being scattered all over in great abundance, casts forth a charming splendour on all sides, so that a sight of this earth is a view of the blessed. It is inhabited by all sorts of animals, and by men, some of whom are cast into the centre of the earth, and others are scattered about the air, as we are above the sea. There are some also that inhabit the isles formed by the air near the continent. For there the air is the same thing that water and sea are here; and the æther does them the same service that the air does to us. Their seasons are so admirably well tempered that their life is much longer than ours, and always free from distempers: and as for their sight, hearing, and all their other senses, and even their intellect itself, they surpass us as far as the æther they breathe in exceeds our gross air for simplicity and purity. They have sacred groves, and temples actually inhabited by the gods, who give evidence of their presence by oracles, divinations, inspirations, and all other sensible signs, and who converse with them. They see the sun and moon without an intervening medium, and view the stars as they are in themselves. And all the other branches of their felicity are proportional to these.

"This is the situation of the earth, and this is the matter of all that surrounds it. All about it there are several abysses in its cavities, some of which are deeper and more open than the country we inhabit; others are deeper, but not so open; and some again have a more extensive breadth, but a lesser depth. And these abysses are bored through in several parts, and have pipes communicating one with another, through which there runs, just as in the caves of Mount Ætna, a vast quantity of water, very large and deep rivers, springs of cold and hot waters, fountains, and rivers of fire, and other rivers of mud, some thinner and some thicker and more muddy, like those torrents of mud and of fire that are cast out from Mount Ætna.

"These abysses are filled with these waters in proportion to their falling out of one into another.

All these sources move both downwards and upwards, like a vessel hung above the earth, which vessel is naturally one, and indeed the greatest of these abysses. It goes across the whole earth, and is open on two sides. Homer speaks of it when he says, 'I'll throw it into the obscure Tartarus, that's a great way from hence, the deepest abyss under the earth.' Homer is not the only author that called this place by the name of Tartarus: most of the other poets did the same.

"All the rivers rendezvous in this abyss, and run out from thence again. Each of these rivers is tinctured with the nature of the earth through which it runs. And the reason of their not stagnating in these abysses is this, that they find no ground, but roll and throw their waters upside down. The air and wind that girds them about does the same, for it follows them when they rise above the earth, and when they descend towards us. And just as in the respiration of animals there is an incessant ingress and egress of air, so the air that mingles with the waters accompanies them in their ingress and egress, and raises raging winds.

"When these waters fall into this lower abyss, they diffuse themselves into all the channels of the springs and rivers, and fill them up, just as if one were drawing up water with two pails, one of which fills as the other empties. For these waters, flowing from hence, fill up our channels; from whence diffusing themselves all about, they fill our seas, rivers, lakes, and fountains. After that they disappear, and diving into the earth, some with a large compass, and others by small turnings, repair to Tartarus, where they enter by other passages than those they came out by, and much lower. Some re-enter on the same side, and others on the opposite to that of their egress; and some again enter on all sides after they have made one or several turns round the earth, like serpents folding their bodies into several rolls; and having gained entrance, rise up to the middle of the abyss, but cannot reach farther, by reason that the other half is higher than the level. They form several very great and large currents; but there are four principal ones, the greatest of which is the outermost of all, and is called the Ocean.

"Opposite to that is Acheron, which runs through the desert place, and diving through the earth, falls into the marsh, which from it is called the Acherusian Lake, whither all souls repair upon their departure from this body; and having stayed there all the time appointed, some a shorter, some a longer time, are sent back to this world to animate beasts.

"Between Acheron and the ocean there runs a third river, which retires again not far from its source, and falls into a vast space full of fire; there it forms a lake greater than our sea, in which the water mixed with mud boils, and setting out from thence all black and muddy, runs along the earth to the end of the Acherusian Lake, without mixing with its waters; and after having made several turnings under the earth, throws itself underneath Tartarus; and this is the flaming river called Phlegethon, the streams whereof are seen to fly up on the earth in several places.

"Opposite to this is the fourth river, which falls first into a horrible wild place, of a bluish colour, called by the name of Stygian, where it forms the formidable Lake of Styx; and after it has tinctured itself with horrible qualities from the water of that lake, dives into the earth, where it makes several turns, and directing its course over against Phlegethon, at last meets it in the Lake of Acheron, where it does not mingle its waters with those of the other rivers, but after it has run its round on the earth, throws itself into Tartarus by a passage opposite to that of Phlegethon. This fourth river is called by the poets Cocytus. Nature having thus disposed of all these things, when the dead arrive at that place whither their Demon leads them, they are all tried and judged, both those that lived a holy and just life, and those who wallowed in injustice and impiety.

"Those who are found to have lived neither entirely a criminal, nor absolutely an innocent life, are sent to Acheron. There they embark in boats, and are transported to the Acherusian Lake, where they dwell, and suffer punishment proportionable to their crimes; till at last being purged and cleansed from their sins, and set at liberty, they receive the recompense of their good actions.

"Those whose sins are incurable, and who have been guilty of sacrilege and murder, or such other crimes, are by a just and fatal destiny thrown headlong into Tartarus, where they are kept prisoners for ever.

"But those who are found guilty of curable (venial) sins, though very great ones, such as offering of violence to their father or mother in a passion, or killing a man, and repenting for it all their lifetime, must of necessity be likewise cast into Tartarus; but after a year's abode there, the tide throws the homicides back into Cocytus, and the parricides into Phlegethon, which draws them into the Acherusian Lake. There they cry out bitterly, and invoke those whom they have killed or offered violence to, to aid them, and conjure them to forgive them, and to suffer them to pass the lake, and give them admittance. If they are prevailed with, they pass the lake, and are delivered from their misery; if not, they are cast again into Tartarus, which throws them back into these rivers; and this continues to be repeated till they have satisfied the injured persons. For such is the sentence pronounced against them.

"But those who have distinguished themselves by a holy life are released from these earthly places, these horrible prisons, and received above into that pure earth where they dwell; and those of them who are sufficiently purged by philosophy live for ever without their body, and are received into yet more admirable and delicious mansions, which I cannot easily describe, neither do the narrow limits of my time allow me to launch into that subject.

"What I told you but now is sufficient, my dear Simmias, to show that we ought to labour all our lifetime to purchase virtue and wisdom, since we have so great a hope and so great a reward proposed to us.

"No man of sense can pretend to assure you that all these things are just as I have said; but all thinking men will be positive that the state of the soul, and the place of its abode after death, is absolutely such as I represent it to be, or at least very near it, provided the soul be immortal; and will certainly find it worth his danger to run the risk; for what danger is more inviting? One must needs be charmed with that blessed hope; and for this reason I have dilated a little upon this subject.

"Every one who during his lifetime renounced the pleasures of the body, who looked upon the appurtenances of the body as foreign ornaments, and siding with the contrary party, pursued only the pleasures of true knowledge, and beautified his soul, not with foreign ornaments, but with ornaments suitable to its nature, such as temperance, justice, fortitude, liberty, and truth;—such a one, being firmly confident of the happiness of his soul, ought to wait peaceably for the hour of his removal, as being always ready for the voyage whenever his fate calls him.

"As for you, my dear Simmias, Cebes, and all you of this company, you shall follow me when your hour comes. Mine is now, and, as a tragical poet would say, the surly pilot calls me aboard; wherefore 'tis time I should go to the bath, for I think 'tis better to drink the poison after I am washed, in order to save the women the trouble of washing me after I am dead."

Socrates having thus spoke, Crito addressed himself to Socrates thus : " Alas, then ! in God's name be it. But what orders do you give me and the rest here present with reference to your children or your affairs, that by putting them in execution we may at least have the comfort of obliging you ? "

" What I now recommend to you, Crito," replies Socrates, " is what I always recommended, that is, to take care of yourselves. You cannot do yourselves a more considerable piece of service, nor oblige me and my family more, than to promise me at this time so to do. Whereas, if you neglect yourselves, and refuse to form your lives according to the model I proposed to you, and follow it, as it were, by the footsteps, all your protestations and offers of service will be altogether useless to me."

" We shall do our utmost, Socrates," replies Crito, " to obey you. But how will you be buried ? "

" Just as you please," says Socrates, " if you can but catch me, and if I do not give you the slip." At the same time, looking upon us with a gentle smile, "I cannot," says he, "compass my end, in persuading Crito that this is Socrates who discourses with you, and methodises all the parts of this discourse; and still he fancies that Socrates is the thing that shall see death by-and-by. He confounds me with my corpse, and in that view asks how I must be buried? And this long discourse that I made to you but now, in order to make it out, that as soon as I shall have taken down the poison I shall stay no longer with you, but shall part from hence, and go to enjoy the felicity of the blessed—in a word, all that I have said for your consolation and mine is to no purpose, but is all lost with reference to him. I beg of you that you will be bail for me to Crito, but after a contrary manner to that in which he offered to bail me to my judges, for he engaged that I would not be gone. Pray engage for me that I shall be no sooner dead but I shall be gone, to the end that poor Crito may bear my death more steadfastly; and when he sees my body burnt or interred, may not despair, as if I suffered great misery, and say at my funeral that

Socrates is interred. For you must know, my dear Crito," says he, turning to him, "that speaking amiss of death is not only a fault in the way of speaking, but likewise wounds the soul. You should have more courage and hope, and say that my body is to be interred. That you may inter as you please, and in the manner that's most comformable to our laws and customs."

Having spoke thus, he rose, and went into the next room to bathe. Crito followed him, and he desired we should attend him. Accordingly we all attended him, and entertained ourselves one while with a repetition and farther examination of what he had said, another while in speaking of the miserable state that was before us. For we all looked upon ourselves as persons deprived of our good father, that were about to pass the rest of our life in an orphan state.

After he came out of the bath, they brought his children to him, for he had three—two little ones, and one that was pretty big: and the women of his family came all in to him. He spoke to them some time in the presence of Crito, gave them their orders, and ordered them to retire, carry his children along with them, and then come back to us. 'Twas then towards sun-setting, for he had been a long while in the little room.

When he came in, he sat down upon his bed, without saying much: for much about the same time the officer of the eleven magistrates came in, and drawing near to him, "Socrates," says he, "I have no occasion to make the same complaint of you that I have every day of those in the same condition; for as soon as I come to acquaint them by orders from the eleven magistrates that they must drink the poison, they are incensed against me and curse me. But as for you, ever since you came into this place, I have found you to be the most even-tempered, the calmest, and the best man that ever entered this prison; and I am confident that at present you are not angry with me; doubtless you are angry with none but those who are the cause of your misfortune. You know them without naming. On this occasion, Socrates, you know what I come to tell you. Farewell! Endeavour to bear this necessity with a constant mind." Having spoke thus, he began to cry, and, turning his back upon us, retired a little. "Farewell, my friend," says Socrates, looking upon him; "I'll follow the counsel thou givest. Mind," says he, "what honesty is in that fellow. During my imprisonment he came often to see me, and conversed with me. He's more worth than all the rest. How heartily he cries for me! Let us obey him with a handsome mien, my dear Crito; if the poison be brewed, let him bring it; if not, let him brew it himself."

"But methinks, Socrates," says Crito, "the sun shines upon the mountains, and is not yet set; and I know several in your circumstances did not drink the poison till a long time after the order was given: that they supped very well, and enjoyed anything they had a mind to. Wherefore I conjure you not to press so hard; you have yet time enough."

"Those who do as you say, Crito," says Socrates, "have their own reasons; they think it is just as much time gained. And I have likewise my reasons for not doing so; for the only advantage I can have by drinking it later is only to make myself ridiculous to myself, in being so foolishly fond of life as to pretend to husband it in the last minute when there's no more to come. Go, then, my dear Crito, and do as I bid you do, and do not vex me any longer."

Whereupon Crito gave the sign to the slave who waited just by. The slave went out, and after he had spent some time in brewing the poison, returned, accompanied by him who was to give it, and brought it all together in one cup. Socrates seeing him come in, "That's very well, my friend," says he; "but what must I do? For you know best, and 'tis your business to direct me."

"You have nothing else to do," says he, "but whenever you have drank it to walk until you find your legs stiff, and then to lie down upon your bed. This is all you have to do." And at the same time he gave him the cup. Socrates took it, not only without any commotion or change of colour or countenance, but with joy; and looking upon the fellow with a steady and bold eye, as he was wont to do, "What do you say of this mixture," says he; "is it allowable to make a drink offering of it?"

"Socrates," replies the man, "we never brew more at once than what serves for one dose."

"I understand you," says Socrates; "but at least is it lawful for me to pray to the gods that they would bless the voyage and render it happy. This I beg of them with all my soul." Having said this he drank it off with an extraordinary calmness and an inexpressible tranquillity.

We had until this time, almost all of us, the power to refrain from tears; but when we saw him drink it off we were no longer masters of ourselves. In spite of all my efforts I was forced to cover myself with my mantle, that I might freely regret my condition; for 'twas not Socrates' misfortune, but my own that I deplored in reflecting what a friend I was bereft of. Crito, who likewise could not abstain from crying, had prevented me, and risen up. And Apollodorus, who scarce ceased to cry during the whole conference, did then howl and cry aloud, insomuch that he moved everybody. Only Socrates himself was not at all moved. On the contrary, he chid them. "What are you doing, my friends?" says he. "What! such fine men as you are! Oh, where is virtue? Was it not for this reason that I sent off those women, for fear they should have fallen into these weaknesses? for I always heard it said that a man ought to die in peace and blessing God. Be easy, then, and show more steadiness and courage." These words filled us with confusion, and obliged us to suppress our tears.

In the meantime he continued to walk, and when he felt his legs stiff he lay down on his back, as the man had commanded him. At the same time the same man that gave him the poison came up to him, and, after looking upon his legs and feet, bound up his feet with all his strength, and asked him if he felt it. He said "No." Then he bound up his legs; and, having carried his hand higher, gave us the signal that he was quite cold. Socrates likewise felt himself with his hand, and told us that when the cold came up to his heart he should leave us. All his lower belly was already frozen. And then uncovering himself (for he was covered),

"Crito," said he (these were his last words), "v
owe a cock to Æsculapius; discharge this vow f(
me, and do not forget it." "It shall be done
said Crito. "But see if you have anything else t
say to us." He made no answer, but after a littl
space of time expired. The man, who was still l
him, having uncovered him, received his last look;
which continued fixed upon him. Crito, seeing that
advanced and shut his mouth and eyes.

This, Echecrates, was the end of our friend, *
man who, beyond all dispute, was the best, an(
most sensible, and the honestest of all our ac
quaintance.

www.ingramcontent.com/pod-product-compliance
Lightning Source LLC
Chambersburg PA
CBHW030821190426
43197CB00036B/711